LIVING EVERY *Single* MOMENT

ANGELA PAYNE

New Hope Publishers
Birmingham, Alabama

New Hope Publishers
P.O. Box 12065
Birmingham, AL 35202-2065
www.newhopepubl.com

Payne, Angela, 1960-
  Living every single moment / Angela Payne.
      p. cm.
  ISBN 1-56309-765-6
  1. Single women—Religious life. 2. Christian women—Religious life.
  I. Title.
  BV4596.S5 P38 2000
  248.8432—dc21
                    99-050937

Unless otherwise noted, Scripture passages are quoted from the NEW AMERICAN STANDARD BIBLE ®, © Copyright The Lockman foundation 1960, 1962, 1963, 1968, 1971, 1972, 1973, 1975, 1977. Used by permission.

Cover design by Dawn Rodgers Design.
Author photo © Edward Badham Photography, Inc.

ISBN: 1-56309-765-6

N004118•0500•7.5M1

James E. Brown
February 15th, 1930–June 3rd, 1999

The ending of one chapter of life as we know it now and the begin
of another life that is forever and ever. It's with love, respect, and h
that I dedicate this book to a man that removed the "step" from our
tionship while exemplifying God's heart of love and compassion t
I miss you, Dad.

Table of Contents

Preface

In writing *Living Every Single Moment*, I sometimes thought I should change it to "Dying Every Single Moment." Or what was really appropriate at times was "Payne in Pain." Whether it is in writing a book or simply getting up in the morning and facing demands of the day, our lives are just like that sometimes!

I recently attended a conference called "Aspiring Women." Ironically, I walked into the event feeling more like an *expired* woman. I had spent the previous night in the Denver airport, returning from a week in Colorado only hours before the conference began. Though I enjoyed the lovely setting nestled in the majestic Rockies, the week had been exhausting for me emotionally and spiritually. I had wrestled with the Lord; and like Jacob, I was limping.

I sat alone in the back of the auditorium, not wanting to talk or to give to others, only longing to absorb some refreshment from the strength of these women gathered for one collective purpose—that they might know God in a deeper way. Though I didn't know these women, their lives touched mine and the Spirit from their hearts flowed quietly into the places of my soul that felt dry and bare. That's one of my favorite things about being female. We are relational even when we don't know one another. There is a time to give and a time to receive. That was my night to receive.

You probably understand what I'm talking about. You have these same emotions, too. Women around the world seem to share them. Because of a passion that I developed years ago for international travel, I have had the opportunity to observe a broad spectrum of women in many settings. I am grateful that my background in nursing has afforded the flexibility and resources to do so. I have noted that women may have vast personality differences, diverse cultural backgrounds, and different languages, but we also have a common thread of emotions that is intricately interwoven in our hearts and spirits.

I hope the common thread of His Spirit will draw our hearts together as you sit with me for a while. Most likely you, as my reader, are a single woman. Perhaps you are single again and are feeling tired, too. I want to give you some of that which has been given to me. Sit back and receive.

In our love...His and mine,

Angela

INTRODUCTION

The ladies' prayer retreat was almost over. It had been a sweet weekend with women of various backgrounds and ages. At the close of worship, two of the girls from my prayer group pulled me aside and asked if we could talk. They were cute girls in their early-to-mid-twenties, who appeared serious and obviously nervous.

Swallowing hard several times and clasping her hands together, the spokesperson of the two finally managed to ask their question. "Angela, are you single?"

"Yes, I am," I answered.

"And you've never been married?" she asked.

"No," I replied.

She took a deep breath and awkwardly blurted out, "And how old are you?"

"I'm thirty," I answered thoughtfully.

By this time, I was amused at her discomfiture. At the disclosure of my age, a sound burst forth from both girls that was an interesting mixture of a wail and an anguished cry with a hint of panic and despair.

With all the dramatic expertise of well-trained actresses, they burst out, "Oh, how do you deal with this?" I assumed that "this" was the fact that I was single at an apparently frightful age. Perhaps I was indeed to be pitied and just didn't know it. I quickly transitioned into the role of the despairing single and nodded my head at my sad state, dropping my eyes to the floor and letting the silence swell the intensity of the moment.

Their eyes were focused on mine as they looked to me for an answer. Knowing I had their complete attention, I replied slowly and quietly. "Girls, the only way I get through this is by seeing my therapist once a week and by taking tranquilizers."

At the looks of horror on their faces, I could not contain my laughter any longer. They looked as if they needed tranquilizers. Still laughing, I put my arms around their shoulders and guided them to a quiet place in a stairwell. We sat down, and I began to share with them where I was in this journey and that this was a time in their lives that was to be enjoyed and fruitful— not wasted while waiting for a husband.

Only weeks before, I had returned from one of the most exciting times of my life in the Middle East. It was during the Gulf War. I encouraged them to pray and begin to seek opportunities to be involved in things that really mattered for eternity. And I reminded them that life without a husband was not to be a time of despair and loneliness but rather of productivity. There are so many areas to be involved in that would make a difference in other lives.

I ran into one of the girls several months later. She told me that after our conversation, she had done two short-term mission trips. Those trips were life-changing for her. My other new friend borrowed my largest suitcase to take on an outreach in Eastern Europe the following summer. I was thrilled to hear how these two young women had responded to the challenge to go beyond their comfort zones, to rise above a summer of going to the beach, meeting for lunch, and praying for a date for the weekend.

I never felt that I would marry at a very early age, and of all the things I have been wrong about, this was not one of them, as evidenced by the fact that it is still me alone in my queen-size bed. I used to have a habit of keeping all my journals and books that I was reading on the other side of my bed; there were never fewer than five books, my prayer journal, my personal journal, bills, etc. It was kind of like sleeping with a desk. My mother would look at all my stuff, shake her head, and say, "It is no wonder you are not married: there is no room for any one else in that bed with you." My bed is now free of books, just to be in a state of preparedness, and my marital status still has not changed.

My two younger sisters and I used to talk of getting married— as sisters do. I would tell them not to wait on me to get married, and they didn't. Dad tried to help me out by saying to one of their suitors,

"I *do* have an older daughter, you know." It was to no avail. At Sister Number One's (Sunnie's) rehearsal dinner, I informed her that I had just been kidding about letting her marry before me. A year later, at Sister Number Two's (Shawn's) rehearsal, I came walking down the aisle wearing a big placard that read "The Last Shall Be First." I was actually thrilled for them and enjoyed being the maid of honor at both of their weddings, joyful in anticipation that mine would be following soon. Sunnie and Shane are about to celebrate their tenth anniversary, Shawn and Brian their ninth. I am not sure when I thought *soon* would be, which leads me to my next inevitable point.

Women are getting married later in life—if at all. I am a statistic I never thought I would be. A statistic that none of us ever wanted to be, most likely. Which of us ever dreamed of being the one at those family and class reunions to whom people would say—always a couple of decibels louder and at least an octave higher—"I can't believe *you* are not married!" I just smile sweetly and say, "I know. I can't believe it either."

I love the comic strip *Cathy*. She and I are kindred spirits. In one of her episodes, she shows up at her friend's house to borrow *something* for her class reunion. As her friend goes to the closet, Cathy informs her that what she needs is not in the closet. She needs to borrow her husband and baby. Well, borrowing a family never crossed my mind, though I did consider asking a friend to loan me his BMW convertible. Incidentally, I went by myself to my twenty-year class reunion and had a fabulous time! Without a husband. Without a baby. Without a BMW. Amazing, isn't it?

One of my greatest desires is to challenge single women to lift their eyes and focus away from the fact that they are single—to embrace opportunities to invest their lives in eternal values. There is not a shortage of things to do, just a shortage of people to do them. One of my favorite sayings for years has been "*Carpe Diem.*" Seize the Day! Notice the exclamation mark; it's there for a reason! This is a time to fill your life with opportunities and adventures that are filled with exclamation points. Not to say that when you are married those opportunities disappear, but there is something about cleaning up diarrhea or changing wet beds that seems to suggest periods or commas instead of exclamation points!

This book is not about men (though there is a chapter on them, and it was my editor's decision to make it the first chapter to get it out of the way); it is about single women. Just as married couples and single parents face challenges unique to their situations, so do single women. Sometimes it's just nice to know you are not a minnow swimming alone in what feels like an ocean of life.

Years ago, Marabel Morgan wrote a best-selling book, *The Total Woman,* that addressed married women from every walk of life. She followed it a few years later with *The Electric Woman.* I have sometimes felt as if I should write *The Short–Circuited Woman.* As a single woman, making decisions that couples usually make together can be challenging, possibly even overwhelming. Taking care of a home and doing things that men traditionally do has been tough, as I am mechanically impaired. There is no "honey do" list in my home. If I don't take the initiative, no one else will. I have just had to learn that Gloria Gaynor is not the only one who can sing "I Will Survive." And if you can't yet sing it, I hope that, after reading this, you will be able to join me in the chorus.

Far beyond the earthly frustrations of playing the dual role of *femme fatale* and handyman are the spiritual frustrations of single women. Some of the issues I want to address may be difficult (who wants to be told there is a possibility she is self-centered?). But I believe my heart is gracious toward women, as I myself am on this journey to a place where I will focus less on myself and concentrate instead on being in alignment with God's will. It is my desire that *Living Every Single Moment* will both challenge and encourage Christian women to love life *now*— not to have an *on hold* mentality until marriage. I want to encourage women honestly to assess their lives and their spiritual foundations. What is the focus of your life, and where are you going? Furthermore, what will you do when you get there? We are instructed in spiritual circles to build a strong and solid foundation. Decisions that we make early in life can help us establish this firm foundation that promotes a healthy relationship with God. Perhaps your foundation has a few chinked or loosened bricks and some of the mortar has been cracked. This is a time to address any of those imperfections.

Writing this book has been like walking down the aisles of the supermarket in my underwear. I feel exposed. After all, most of my material has been drawn from eighteen years of personal journals, which up to this point I have guarded with my life. Now I have opened their tear-and coffee-stained pages for you to share in my laughter and sorrows, triumphs and heartaches. There are some pages of this *agony and ecstasy* that I would rewrite if I could. I would tear them out if that would change things, but that won't work, for they are, after all, written on the pages of my heart. Perhaps in the transparency of my failures and victories you will be inspired to write in the journals of your heart with a little more insight than I have.

Keep in mind that the tragedy of single people lies not in the singleness itself, but rather in the time that they waste waiting for it to end. At this moment in our lives and for all the days that follow, we must learn to appreciate the sovereign gift of the *here and now*. When the reality of eternity jumps between the right and left ventricles of your heart, your whole focus and perspective on life will change. And you will know assuredly that you can stop worrying about what the future might hold for you. Instead, busy yourself about your Father's business, confident that He will be busy about the things that pertain to you. It's time to stop living for the future. Live now—every single and wonderful moment of your life!

Chapter One

MAN IS A PIECE OF WORK

Shakespeare (*Hamlet* Act 2)

As I walked into the nurses station one morning, a co-worker, who regularly rolled her eyes at my high standards for a husband, presented me with a gift. It was a picture of three female skeletons with high heels and purses sitting on a park bench. The caption below the picture read, "Waiting for the Perfect Man." Admittedly, I laughed with my cackling colleague. After all, we girls know that there really is such a thing as the perfect man…he is somewhere out there with the perfect woman.

Elisabeth Elliot has said of her husband, Lars, that she is married to a sinner, and so is he. It is the same for every other spouse in the world. Yet, most of us single Christian women sinners seem to want one of these male sinners. The topic of *men* inevitably arises at any gathering of single women, Christian or not, and it certainly cannot be excluded from a book by a single female. Oh, the hours that we have spent discussing those descendants of Adam! In preparing this manuscript, I have recalled many such hours filled with sweet and tender thoughts, perplexed and anguished cries, frustration, and indignation. And believe it or not, writing about men is more emotionally challenging than crying about them!

This chapter is not going to be a tirade against men. I find myself rather fond of them. Some of my favorite people are men with whom I have enjoyed positive relationships for years. Most of them are now married, and I am grateful that our friendships have remained and now extend to their wives and children. Thus anything I may say here will be written from what I believe is a healthy and whole heart and not from cynicism.

In pouring over these journals of my life, I look back and see where I made some wise decisions pertaining to issues of my heart as a single woman. I am also reminded of some unwise choices. I wish I had at times been more cautious with my heart, established a few more boundaries, and not have been so trusting, especially of my own emotions. Having spent countless hours listening and praying with friends in their desire to understand a relationship or to be healed from the aftermath of a broken one, I know I have not been alone. We so easily allow men to become distractions from God's direction for our lives. These distractions can produce headaches and heartaches.

So what's a girl to do? Avoid men altogether? Heaven forbid. But we must not approach them as our secular society dictates we should. When our hearts, emotions, and desires are yielded to God, we will learn how to maintain a healthy Christian perspective in our desire for male companionship and our attitudes toward men. Only then will we be able to effectively ease the distraction of men and keep our focus where it should be.

Understanding Tears

It had been one of those years where more money than I had was being spent on bridesmaid dresses and wedding gifts. A nice refreshing fall had just started, and I was looking forward to some autumn hiking with my adventuresome friend. She had been spending some time with a really nice guy who—she kept insisting—was *just a friend*. During an especially challenging week at work, I had received three phone calls from close friends announcing their engagements. Although happy for them, I was beginning to feel a little left out. I had worked Friday night and was getting ready to go to bed Saturday morning when the phone rang. Instead of phoning to arrange a hike, my kindred outdoors companion was calling with news of a diamond ring. I hurt her feelings with my outburst of tears—a torrential flood of them. Then I got in the bathtub and cried for thirty more minutes. That was ten years ago, and

I have never had that reaction again. Not yet, anyway. The Lord has governed me with His grace for every wedding since then, and it's always nice to check someone off that particular prayer list.

Other parts of being single are disappointing at times, too. For me, one of the most difficult things about not being married is not having children. As I was driving to North Carolina to meet my second niece, just a few hours after her birth, I had to come to a place of spiritual surrender. "Father," I prayed, "if it is your will, I will walk away from the desire for marriage and children forever, and will focus on being a wonderful aunt to these two nieces You have given to me." It was really a place of the Cross for me, and holding little Lydia for the first time was bittersweet.

In this place of surrender, is the desire gone? Not in the least. I still hope to change my own baby's diapers some day. But just as I have confidence in a loving Father who directs my steps, this also includes my heart and all of its longings. It is *only* because of that truth that I can have peace.

I often find myself needing to renew this confidence and to refocus on the Lord as my source of true joy. Recently I was in my car at a stoplight near my home when I saw a mother and little girl walk out of a dance studio. With awe in my voice, I leaned out the window and called to the little girl in her tutu: "Are you a *real* ballerina?" She took her finger out of her mouth long enough to look up shyly, smile, and duck her head. I drove away and promptly burst into tears. Those kinds of tears are okay. It's not a matter of feeling sorry for yourself; it's a matter of grieving. My heart can so identify with the verse in Proverbs 13:12: "Hope deferred makes the heart sick."

In this world, there is pain. Singles feel the pain of being alone. Couples often know the pain of infertility. Some parents have the pain of losing a child or watching one suffer. People all over the world experience incredible painful events, both physically and emotionally. Life just sometimes turns out answers you wouldn't have chosen on a multiple-choice test. The rest of Proverbs 13:12 reads, "but desire fulfilled is the tree of life." In the middle of pain or disappointment, we can know the hope of our desires fulfilled, though it may be in a way we didn't expect. God has a much bigger picture of our lives than we can see or feel at times.

I have walked in so many wonderful and fulfilled days when I could say, "Who have I in heaven but thee, and there is none upon earth that I desire besides thee." And then there have been those moments that I was filled with fear, doubt, and longings all intertwined together. Most of us as single women have had those moments. I remember a specific dark night when it was late and I couldn't sleep. Emotions like the waves of a storm at sea began to sweep over me. Thoughts of being alone the rest of my life without a husband or children relentlessly pounded against my soul. I was shrouded in fear. Dark waters flooded my heart, and I felt as if I was drowning. I couldn't breathe. Finally, in the early morning hours I called my mother. I could not talk for the sobs yet she understood, and she prayed. The dark waters of my night began to recede and I sensed the quiet, soothing calm that follows after the storm. With the morning light, I opened my Bible and began reading from the Psalms. I noted a commentary in my Bible by Charles Spurgeon where he defined tears as "liquid prayer." He then outlined his study on tears and the role they play in a spirit of brokenness and intercession. My tears had not been wasted; the dark despair of that troubled night was exchanged for comfort and peace.

In times of tears and brokenness we must not allow our hearts to become desperate and consequently compromise our beliefs. We all could have been married to someone by now, or at least *something* that resembled a man. It's most likely there have been some wonderful men in all of our pasts—men that would have made fabulous husbands, and now *are* fabulous husbands…to someone else.

I was recently asked why opportunities in the past had not worked for me. Quite simply, I didn't have peace *or* he didn't have peace. And of course, there is the one guy who said, "There're just no sparks." My doting and eager grandmother offered to give him a firecracker.

No matter how much you would like for a relationship to work, if there isn't any peace in your heart or the attraction, you need to make an exit. It doesn't matter how wonderful he is or that you appear to make "the perfect" couple. Let it be *The End* of a potential Harlequin Romance without trying to write another chapter. When I have wandered off the path of peace, so to speak, I have unexpectedly walked into a few potholes, ravines, and sewage drains. Stay on the path of His divine guidance that is overshadowed by His peace. It's safe. And if for a moment you find you're self-rationalizing in issues of character, it's time to jump off the Love Boat and swim to shore.

On the opposite end of the spectrum, you must trust that God is leading Christian men as well. Sometimes it's not a character issue, it's simply not God's will and the man is obedient to end a relationship. If your heart has known the pain of what feels like rejection, ask your Father to let you see it as His protection. This has changed my whole perspective on pain in the past and even very recently. Sometimes you have to remember this with your head until it is eventually absorbed in your heart. A sovereign God will without a doubt direct a man and woman who are committed to God's plan and purposes.

G-rated in an R-rated World

Working in secular settings and maintaining moral standards can set you up as a great source of entertainment for your co-workers. Let them laugh, and even laugh with them! You don't have to defend your choice, and you certainly don't have to act like the "pristine paragon of chastity" while maintaining a lifestyle of sexual purity. The reality of our "Nineties Sexual Generation" is that the world is in complete chaos when it comes to morals and absolutes. There are times when you might need to draw your boundaries with men who still think they can have a "free for all" with women in the workplace. You can either remind them that you have protection through sexual harassment laws or you can be creative. Creative boundaries are much more memorable!

I was working at a new hospital and had made rounds on several occasions with one of our surgeons. He had taken liberties in making what I suppose he meant to be flattering comments to me. One day, the two of us happened to be alone on the elevator. All at once, he pinched my thigh and gave a look that said he was going for more before we reached the sixth floor. It so caught me off guard that I burst out laughing, which I think terribly deflated his ego. No more pinches. No more comments.

On another occasion, after several weeks of comments and heavy breathing in my ear from another male co-worker, I had had it. *Really* had it. Particularly since my repeated requests that he keep his comments to himself seemed only to have worsened the situation. This time when he made one of his hot and profane comments, I took a deep breath, calmly looked in his eyes, quietly said, "Big boy, you just really need to *cool off*," and emptied my glass of ice water on him. I turned my back to him and tried to ignore the commotion behind me, continuing to chart with my trembling hand! I could hear him spewing and cursing and out of the corner of my eye saw the other nurses scatter. He changed not only his scrubs that day but also his attitude. That was the end to the obscene remarks or heavy breathing in my ear.

I have learned there are no international boundaries between men, women, and hormones. The only difference is skin color and languages. These experiences have broadened my observations with many types of men. Some have been helpful, and some have been irritating. During the Gulf War, I was in Jerusalem working as the hospitality coordinator for a prayer ministry. On a particularly hot day, I walked into town for eggs and milk. I was beginning a long climb up the Mount of Olives where I lived when an Israeli soldier stopped and asked if I would like a lift to the top of the mountain. Grateful for his kindness, I naively got in. We had gone about two blocks when he asked if I would like to go with him to a nearby hotel. My temperature gage accelerated to a boiling point, and I told him exactly what I thought of his *kindness*. I started getting out of the jeep while it was still moving and was about to storm away when I saw my pail of eggs. What a marvelous idea! As I was getting ready to aim for his head, I heard that "Whoa!" from above. In my mind's eye, I could picture the Lord calling a host of angels and saying, "Go and stop her!"

Now in the instance of that friendly opportunistic soldier, it was quite easy for me to turn down his rather impassioned request. I wasn't the least bit tempted to cross the sacred boundaries of chastity. I only wanted to throw eggs. But what if I had been tempted, and what about when I am tempted (please note *present* tense)?

Some of us mistakenly think as we get older that we become less vulnerable to sexual temptation. If anything, as I get older I find my feelings for love and romance have intensified. (I am *definitely* having that feeling that I am standing in the grocery store in my underwear.) Feelings, desires, and the longing to be touched and held are all part of who we are as emotional and normal women. But whether we like it or not, we don't have a choice about sexual purity, unless we want to suffer the emotional wounding and physical consequences of intimacy outside of marriage.

I was in my early teens when I made my official declaration for virginity. I boldly and confidently stated that I would courageously and valiantly turn away from all sexual desire, temptation, and passion until that most glorious, sacred, and anticipated wedding night. I didn't know *The Night* was going to stretch into what now appears to be infinity. Somewhere along the years, I unknowingly perched myself on a self-imposed pedestal of virtue. And there I sat sanctimoniously shunning all temptation. I think I must have had latent puberty because it wasn't until my late twenties and early thirties that my little pedestal began to totter and sway, and I found myself hanging on for dear life. You know the abstinence rings that parents are now giving their kids as a reminder for sexual purity? Honest truth, my mother gave me one when I was thirty— I'm still wearing it. I can say it is by His grace and not my sheer will power that I haven't fallen off my pedestal. In fact, I took myself from my self-imposed perch and now I sit humbly at His feet knowing how quickly I can fall. I am always ever mindful of my need for Him. And *that* is a good place to be.

It is wise to assess our weak points. Yes, there is His abundant grace, but we have to be wise in relational decisions. Because most women are more feeling and emotionally oriented, we can be more susceptible to misguided romantic feelings. When we gage a situation by our feelings, we open ourselves up to poor judgment in life's most important decisions. Our feelings are often disloyal to truth. And if you remember the song "Feelings" that many of us sang at our high school prom; it is true; especially the *wailing* and *whoaa* part. I have a whole repertoire of instances where my *feelings* could have gotten me into trouble.

On our way home from a mission trip to Japan, my sister and I stopped in Hawaii. It was one of the most romantic places I could have ever imagined. But I said I would never go back there again without being married because by the end of the week, some thoroughly impossible candidates were beginning to look good to me. *Feelings.*

One year when I was in Germany, I took a train to visit the concentration camp of Dacchau. Unfortunately, it was the wrong train. On it, however, was an Australian "knight in shining armor" who not only came to the rescue of this directionally challenged "damsel in distress" but also accompanied me to Dacchau and an Oktoberfest. We enjoyed each other's conversation so much that we lost track of time and nearly missed my return train. We arrived at the railway station just in time for him to lift me and my backpack into the train. Taking my hands, he looked deeply into my eyes, put his business card in my jacket, and said with a charming Dundee accent, "Write to me. Blessings." He stepped off the train, and the doors closed. I leaned against the wall, swooning at the sheer romance of the moment and watched his silhouette fade in the shadow of the full moon. A few days later, I had lost his card. A sweet, fickle romantic encounter. *Feelings.*

I have a decided weakness for men who love children. There was a man I had never paid a bit of attention to until I saw him rolling on the floor, covered in kids. Then he had my attention. But after he got up and we began talking incompatibly, my maternal hormones returned to normal. *Feelings.*

In my experience, the only nice thing about being uptight about a guy is that my weight is usually what I want it to be. The perpetual knot in my stomach, though not pleasant, is good for my tight jeans. I have a pair that I call my *love jeans.* I have only been able to wear them twice in my life. They are too tight right now, which is indicative of my romantic status. *Feelings.*

In order to avoid being controlled by irresponsible feelings, it is important for Christian singles to establish the kind of mate they desire, as well as their reasons for wanting to be married. These reasons should go beyond the obvious desires for companionship, children, and so on. In my desire to be identified with a strong Christian man, it is because I know the most spiritually powerful marriage is a couple yielded and submitted together to His will. Last year, I was in Oxford, England, browsing in an old bookstore, when I found the following prayer by Temple Gairdner. I was deeply touched by the heart cry of this prayer. To me it fully reflects what our desire should be for a godly mate.

That I may come near to her, draw me nearer to thee than to her;
that I may know her, make me to know thee more than her;
that I may love her with the perfect love of a perfectly whole heart,
cause me to love thee more than her
and most of all. Amen Amen
That nothing may be between me and her, be thou between us,
every moment.
That we may be constantly together, draw us into separate
loneliness with thyself.
And when we meet breast to breast, my God, let it be on thine own.
Amen Amen[1]

—Temple Gairdner, 1873-1928, before his marriage

If young women prayerfully set standards for a godly husband, it would eliminate confusion and wasted time. I would encourage you prayerfully to ask the Lord to show you what kind of characteristics and qualities He wants you to have in a husband. Focus on character issues. Get to know godly male role models, especially father figures, both in person and through Christian biographies. If there is someone who has caught your attention, ask yourself this question: "Does he love the Lord Jesus more than he loves me?" That question has been in my heart as long as I can remember. Don't waste your time on someone with a lot of potential; character issues are the key. And most likely if they are not there now, they won't be there any time soon. Incidentally, don't even think about "missionary dating." Most of those attempts end in disaster.

A biblical concept for *courtship* is emerging again that is worth noting. It replaces "casual dating" which often leads to "confused dating." In courtship, there is a defined and stated purpose in getting to know one another. The concept is based on mutual respect and honor for one another's hearts, not only in words but physically. You have a desire to want the best for that person without selfish motives. The central focus is to know God's will for two lives in relation to marriage rather than in just having another relationship. It's a very nice alternative.

I personally began praying for my husband when I was a teenager. Though I don't know all the details of this man—especially his whereabouts—I know the kinds of unnegotiable character qualities he needs to possess. I hope he'll have some more debatable personality traits. During my second year of college, I described my ideal husband in my journal. He had the spiritual life of Billy Graham, the romance of Cary Grant, the sweetness of Francis of Assisi, and the humor of Hawkeye on *Mash*. (Is there such a man?) One thing is certain, if the Lord has planned for me to marry, He is well aware of this man's location and identity. My four-year-old niece recently asked me if my husband were in heaven. I laughed replying, "Caroline, *that's* where he is! And I've been looking for him down here!" The thought of being married to an angel sounds kind of sweet—Angela and her Angel.

Whether you are in love with an angel or a man, what if you are beyond the stage of *feelings* and are in a courtship or dating someone? This relationship *finally* has substance to it and you might even be engaged. It's easy to walk away from temptation if you aren't interested, but what if there is someone whom you do care about? When our heart and emotions are involved, problems can develop. My pedestal started rocking and reeling a few years ago and I realized that I better make a plan of escape while I could think clearly. As I have told the kids that I have worked with in the Abstinence Program, after the back seat windows get steamed up, it's a little too late to have any rationality. You have to think and plan now while your perception gage is clear and not steamy. Even as adult women. Here are some plans that I have made.

My mind is creative enough without the assistance of Hollywood. I have to be extremely careful about what movies I see or books that I read. Some may call it prudish; I call it hormonal wisdom.

Accountability is a wonderful tool in helping you make wise decisions. I have two close friends and a couple in my church that I have made myself accountable to in the issue of sexual purity.

Don't allow yourself to get into a situation that can get out of control. When I was in Hong Kong, I ordered a kimono from the most handsome and charming man I had ever met— up to that point of my life anyway. Merely standing next to this Englishman literally made me dizzy. He had a magnetizing presence about him that made me swoon like some adolescent teenager. The next day I returned to his shop to pick up my purchase and again experienced the same sort of heart palpitations and flushed face. Maybe it was some exotic cologne he was wearing but I most definitely could not think clearly with him looking down into my eyes. He asked me to dine with him in an elegant restaurant overlooking this very romantic city. The restaurant just happened to be above a hotel. I knew exactly what his intentions were. I didn't trust him, and I sure didn't trust me. Though terribly attracted to his smooth demeanor, I declined and dragged myself out of his store. Your greatest strength can be that you know your weakness. I was aware of how weak I was that night. That was a fleeting moment of temptation, and I knew I would be back to normal after I walked away. *It's even more important to stay out of tempting situations with someone you know and care about.*

There are certain climates that I need to stay away from with single men. For example, a nice blazing fire and the beach at night are real romance jump-starters for me. These two environments provoke *feelings* that could easily confuse issues.

In addition to your own plans, a desire and commitment from both people in a relationship is important to remain morally pure. You've got to be on the same team with the same goal—not to defraud one another. Let me share a very true and very honest story with you that I believe will be invaluable in my point. It was a snowy night in a place far away from my home. I was just getting ready to say goodnight to someone I cared about very much. Without warning, a heavy snow and ice storm started. You can roll your eyes around all you like at what I'm about to say, but we were snowed in! The chalet was at a very high elevation, and there was no safe way for him to get down an extremely steep and icy mountain.

It was just like a Hollywood script, only it was real. We were a perfect opportunity for disaster or grace. Two adults in a romantic chalet in front of a lovely fire trying to stay warm. For us, this was such an important time that we could not cloud the purpose of our relationship with any physical issues. I will always respect him for his integrity shown that night and marvel at my own! Incidentally, he was able to make it down the mountain in a few hours. This is certainly not the way MGM would have written the rest of the script! If we will just cooperate with the leading and protection of the Holy Spirit, He will make a way of escape in those tempting moments.

Matchmakers Anonymous

You will find as you get older that friends, family members, and co-workers consider it their mission to diagnose why you are not yet married and to prescribe remedies accordingly. In my case, these pseudo-psychologists have speculated that my single condition stems from my outrageously lofty standards, my unwillingness to submit to a husband, the desire for a perfect man, my independence, etc. Such words can be wounding. If they have been said to you, let them be as arrows that bounce off the shield of the Lord's protection. And if there are areas to change, the Lord will bring them to your attention.

Sometimes the radical treatments prescribed by these well-meaning specialists can be even distressing or sometimes amusing. One day I was visiting my Aunt Myrtle. Most predictably, she leaned over with that sparkle in her eighty-year-old eyes and asked, "Angela, is there anything new?"

I knew exactly what she meant and nodded my usual "No."

"Maybe this will help," she said.

Smiling proudly as if she had just given me a magical cure-all, she handed me a clipping entitled "Hot Spots for Meeting Mr. Right." Among other places the article listed work, health clubs, church, homes and parties of mutual friends, weddings, conferences, public transportation, bus stations, laundromats, supermarkets, and airports. I read the list and jumped up to leave.

"Where are you going? You just got here." Aunt Myrtle asked.

"I'm going to go sit in the airport," I answered, as I jokingly shut the door behind me.

Our pseudo-psychologists mean well. Sometimes we simply have to laugh at all their efforts to assist us out of our woeful single status. My friend Judy is *sure* my husband is a guy she knows in Seattle. I haven't yet met him, but he sounds like the making of another great movie! Admittedly, some wonderfully matched couples have actually met on blind dates. Therefore, I dare not toss the matchmaking process as a whole. Nonetheless, I rarely accept blind dates anymore. They are kind of like five extra pounds or bounced checks—I can do without them.

Though your matchmaking friends mean well, don't trust them! Whether or not you are desperate, people will sometimes assume you are. My advice is to take a cell phone on any blind date, just in case you need to be rescued. On one memorable blind date, the guy kept taking me to places where his old girlfriends used to live, driving his Bronco like a tank plowing over everything in its path. The more he talked about his girlfriends, the more intense he got. I think he had a lot of unresolved anger, but I was not about to be Nancy counselor. The only nice thing about the evening was that it ended.

We all have our stories, but the best one happened to a friend whom I will call Tracy, since that is her name. Wanting to surprise her, her date would only give hints concerning their upcoming evening. They spoke a few days before the event and from all clues she thought they were going to the symphony. A classical pianist, she was thrilled that they had common musical interests. Mr. Sophisticated. Mr. Sensitive. Maybe even Mr. Right. He drove her to Atlanta, and *surprise*! He had bought front-row seats at a tractor pull! I thought I had some war stories, but as far as I'm concerned, she gets the prize.

Of course, there are a few men who may tell their tales of woe in remembering me. I recall one evening which started out with a big rainstorm. A married couple had invited me on a double date with the new doctor from a small town nearby. Who knew that my full skirt was flapping in the rain the entire fifty-minute drive to the restaurant? I got out of the car and my whole backside was wet. Fortunately, the restroom was equipped for such emergencies with an electric hand dryer. Backing up against the hot air, I had blistered my bottom by the time my dress was dry. As we were walking to our table, I slipped on an incline and landed on my blistered bottom. Looking down at me on the floor, my doctor date said, "Sorry, my specialty is family practice, not orthopedics." The old adage applied again, "All's well that ended."

In addition to setting us up on blind dates, some of our loved ones (like Aunt Myrtle) will encourage dating services and singles events. Bringing in my mail one afternoon, I recognized the handwriting of a very close friend and knew it was her wedding invitation. For many years she and I had asked God to bring about this day. I clasped the envelope and thanked the Father aloud. The next piece of mail I opened started out like this: "Tired of singles bars and blind dates? You can choose a more dignified alternative. *Great Expectations* offers you the opportunity to meet interesting selective singles in the privacy of a relaxed unpressured atmosphere." I was struck by the stark contrast between the invitation and the ad. Leave *Great Expectations* to Dickens, I thought, as I tossed the flyer in the trash.

Whereas a dating service is not something I would necessarily recommend, I do think singles events provide wonderful opportunities for meaningful friendships. I loved the singles events in college and the few years following. However, if you are going to these events with a marriage resume in your purse, or with a "male Geiger stick" in hand,

I would suggest you stay at home and read a good book until you get this issue settled in your heart. Relax and enjoy this season of your life. It may stretch out longer than you want it to, but be assured in knowing that He will be much more creative and romantic in your matchmaking than you could ever dream of.

Men: Who Needs Them Anyway? We do!

I experienced my first real heartbreak at an age when most of my friends had been married for years. Wondering if I could ever trust myself to love again, I discovered a meaningful passage by C.S. Lewis in *The Four Loves.*

> *To love at all is to be vulnerable. Love anything, and your heart will certainly be wrung and possibly be broken. If you want to make sure of keeping it intact, you must give your heart to no one. Not even an animal.*
>
> *Wrap it carefully round with hobbies and little luxuries; avoid all entanglements; lock it up safe in the casket or coffin of your selfishness. But in that casket—safe, dark, motionless, airless—it will change. It will not be broken; it will become unbreakable, impenetrable, irredeemable. The alternative to tragedy, or at least to the risk of tragedy, is damnation. The only place outside heaven where you can be perfectly safe from all the dangers and perturbations of love is Hell.*[2]

Lewis's words pierced my mind and helped my hurt to heal. The book of Proverbs admonishes us to guard our hearts diligently. But I had to follow this advice—as it pertained to men—without becoming bitter or closed.

One reason I kept the door of my heart shut to some men in the past was the proverbial fear of rejection. I felt that if they really got to know me in my imperfections they would lose interest in me. My heart's desire for a husband has always been that he would see me in my weaknesses and flaws and still love me. Of course, I am not alone. Many of you feel the same way. So did Ruth Bell Graham, as indicated in the poem from *Sitting by My Laughing Fire* that she endearingly wrote before her marriage to Billy Graham.

God,
let me be all he ever dreamed
of loveliness and laughter.
Veil his eyes a bit
because there are so many little flaws;
somehow, God,
please let him see
only the bride I long to be
remembering ever after-
I was all he ever dreamed
of loveliness and laughter.[3]

Just as it is every woman's heart to know unconditional love, so we must be willing to love unconditionally. Let's face it; a lot of great guys out there fear rejection too. And they may be praying the prayer for us that Billy Graham probably prayed for Ruth. To be drawn to someone's heart first is not typical in many relationships because of the focus on physical attraction. A friend told me of her neighbor that got married recently. Instead of a diamond ring she got breast implants and lipo-suction. In telling my brother-in-law the story he grinned and said, "I can hear her husband saying, 'Honey, I will love you unconditionally as soon as the swelling and bruising goes away'." How's that for starting a life of marital bliss and unconditional love!

Mutual honor should also have a place of importance in male-female relationships. About three years ago, I was on what I called a Jane Austen roll, reading her books while the videos of them were still rewinding in my VCR. A few days after I had finished the Austen marathon, I received a phone call from a man that I had known for sev-eral years. We chatted pleasantly for a few minutes before he voiced his reason for calling. He was going to be in town and wanted me to join him for dinner. Happy to hear from him, I gladly accepted, and we confirmed a date and time. Before he hung up, he said, rather matter-of-factly, "Angela, I want to be entirely honest with you and tell you that I am corresponding with someone from another state." As silly as it may have sounded, I replied with what I meant to be a compliment: "You rank as a Jane Austen kind of man. Honest and honoring, not wanting to mislead. It's also called decent behavior. Thank you." I said. We had a wonderful dinner, two friends with no presumptions or false expectations. Don't settle for less than honorable men who treat you with respect physically and emotionally.

We women have often been told that a man who doesn't respect a woman's heart is not worthy of her attention. The reverse is true as well. It is just as important for us to be honoring to men as for them to be to us. I wish I did not have to admit this, but I have acted disrespectfully toward someone's heart. I met with him a couple of years ago to talk and to return a very expensive gift that I had not felt right about taking. Because of my foolish efforts to change him, I had wounded him and caused deep pain. Completely broken, I despised myself at the realization of the hurt I had inflicted on him and asked his forgiveness. Kindly and graciously, he forgave me.

Men:
You CAN live with them and you CAN live without them!
There have been a few days when I have been cynical toward men and perhaps for legitimate reasons. If I allowed myself to focus on some of the negative characteristics that I have seen in the typical Christian male of this century, I would indeed despair. On the other hand, many men are trustworthy and filled with integrity. The fact that most are now married is beside the point. They have brothers. They have friends. They have widowed fathers! Take hope!

The gift of laughter in the midst of difficult times is indeed a great blessing. But we also must learn from hurtful situations and seek not to repeat our own mistakes or those of others. In particular, experience and observation in the area of romance can teach us how to guard our hearts against disappointment and bitterness and how to ease the distractions of men.

One evening I had dinner with a friend who felt perplexed in a *semiromantic* relationship. "Well, I think it's progressing," she said slowly, wrinkling her face with a confused look. "He calls about once a week. But, you know that's his personality. He's just really slow. It's not that we have kissed or held hands, but he acts so affectionate."

Same story multiplied a million times. I believe there is a kiss to your heart that is more intimate than any physical kiss. That little gem of a proverb is worth noting, "Charm is deceitful" (Prov. 31:30). A man being warm and friendly is not in the same category as charm. When the charm wears off, you have nothing left but character or the lack of it.

A few years ago some friends introduced me to a handsome, charming, and interesting guy. Over a three-week period we went on a few casual outings together, and enjoyed some light, fun talks. One day, he mentioned that he had seen *Sense and Sensibility* three times.

"*Really?* You really liked it?" I asked.

"Oh, I loved it," he said. "It is one of the most emotionally intense movies I have ever seen."

Like a big ole catfish, I was hooked. All I needed was to be reeled in. A sensitive man in touch with his feelings, and I was looking at him. At the end of that sweet and romantic evening, he didn't say good-bye; instead, he looked deeply into my eyes and said, "I will call you soon." I never heard another word from him.

Some men seem to be as cool as a breeze in Antarctica one hour and as warm as the summer sun the next. They are kind of like the wind. You can hear and feel them, but you sure can't tell what direction they are going. Because of this tendency, many women waste a lot of precious time and emotional energy on one-sided romances. When a man's actions communicate interest, but he refuses to verbalize his intentions or any commitment, remember that he is a person and not a radio: you can't just turn down the volume. Instead of using your uncanny female ability to create a lot of *romantic imaginations* about what his actions might mean, walk away. If he has intentions of pursuing you, he will.

It's worth pointing out that women have unusual creative abilities when it comes to romance. I call it the "Art of Delilah." We can pray with such earnestness and think we are being led by the Lord with our sweet and coy wiles of manipulation. Ask the Lord to remove presumptuous thoughts from your heart. Desire to have pure motives. In addition, as women we can so easily set ourselves up for hurt and disaster by doing what we do so well— talking. The more you talk about your feelings the more they are intensified. It's very simple. Keep quiet about the issues of your heart and you will have fewer regrets. (Oh, that I had read this book ten years ago.)

It shames me to admit that I have wasted vast amounts of both emotional and physical energy on non-committal men. Perhaps to fulfill my feminine need to nurture, I have washed clothes, cleaned toilets, baked cookies, and mopped floors like some sort of surrogate housewife, and I literally cherished the opportunity to do these things. Looking back, it makes me think I must have overdosed on artificial sweetener and knocked off more than a few brain cells. These charming and endearing males loved my affirmation, companionship, and cooking. Why did they need to marry me?

Hello, girls! This is a wake-up call! No more cleaning or cooking for men who are not our husbands! And what is it with us that when we get warm feelings about someone we immediately want to bake chocolate chip cookies for him? I hereby proclaim an official *ban on baking chocolate chip cookies for single men!* There are other outlets for those nurturing needs. Bake for your neighbors, new babies, the library bake sale or shut-ins, but *not* for men whom you want to impress.

Your Father Doeth ALL Things Well

Especially as we get older, discouraging thoughts may invade our minds: You missed it with him; he missed it when he married her; if only you had gone on that ski trip. This is just a creative attempt of Satan to play with your mind and heart. "I know whom I have believed,

25

and am persuaded that He is able to keep that which I have committed unto Him" (2 Tim. 1:12). This verse includes your heart and any future husband. Recommit your heart and future to God in complete trust. There is not a safer place to be.

This can be one of the most fulfilling and meaningful seasons of your life. Any single woman looking for her fulfillment exclusively in marriage will certainly know great disappointment. If we are not fulfilled in our lives before marriage, we certainly will not be after the honeymoon. This is a time in our lives to focus on a fulfilling and intimate relationship with Jesus, not just in our minds but in our hearts. Then our lives will reflect to others that we know Him—that we *really* know Him.

As an obstetrical nurse I have coached many women in labor to have a focal point in the room. The purpose of this activity is for maternity patients to concentrate on the object instead of the pain. On a spiritual level, the focal point of our lives has to be the Lord Jesus Christ and His sovereignty. We don't need to be blinded by our emotions, tears, joys, possibilities, goose bumps, chill bumps, or glow-in-the-dark feelings. It must be on Him alone that our trust is established. He directs our steps and hearts and withholds no good thing from us. Surely the God who keeps the universe in place is able to keep our lives and all that pertains to our hearts on course. His loving gaze is always upon you. He sees you while you are awake. He looks upon you when you are asleep. He is forever near you—every single moment.

¹ Appleton, George, ed., *The Oxford Book of Prayer* (New York:Oxford University Press, 1985).
²Lewis, C.S., *The Four Loves* (Orlando: Harcourt, Brace, Jovanovich, 1960), 169.
³Graham, Ruth Bell, *Sitting By My Laughing Fire* (Waco: Word Books, 1977).

Chapter Two

KEEPER OF THE SPRINGS

More than sixty years ago Helen Wright, a concert pianist in her mid-twenties, walked down the aisle to meet her groom. Beaming with joy, this devout bride silently thanked God for her Christian husband, unaware of what lay ahead. Within a year, Helen gave birth to a sick baby who died only hours later. The young, devastated mother never even saw her infant. As she cried in her hospital bed, she heard the Lord speak softly to her spirit: "Do not cry, Helen; I will be your Husband and I will give you many spiritual children." Helen quietly pondered these words in her heart.

One day not long afterwards, her husband threw his Bible across the room and walked out of her life. Her world shattered, Helen comforted herself with the words God had spoken to her in the hospital, considering them not only a promise but also a calling. She left a teaching position at a prestigious liberal arts college and spent the next thirty-five years teaching music at a Bible school and doing volunteer work at a home for troubled girls on weekends. And she saw God's promise to her unfold.

Today Miss Helen, still vivacious in her eighties, is the spiritual mother of literally hundreds of children from all backgrounds. I first became one of them about fifteen years ago. Upon hearing that she'd been a bridesmaid at age seventy-three, I was determined to get to know this lady. So as a birthday present to myself that year, I called her and arranged for us to meet later that week.

Since then, she has influenced me greatly, consistently refocusing me on the Lord when my vision has become a little blurred. It was she who really sparked my desire to continue with my journals. Often she has presented me with new ones, encouraging me to write the new chapters of my life upon their blank pages. She has also been most instrumental in leading me to have quiet times and to learn to listen.

In addition to mentoring me spiritually, Miss Helen has been a spunky friend whose company I have thoroughly enjoyed. On her eighty-second birthday I covered the entire doorframe of her apartment with decorated banner paper so that when she opened the door, she could see nothing but the banner. I knocked hard on the door, unsure of what her reaction to this practical joke would be. When she opened to a wall of paper, she laughed out loud and started beating her way out! If she weren't afraid to climb a ladder, I dare say she'd try this trick herself on one of her octogenarian neighbors!

Miss Helen is what Ingrid Trobish would call a "keeper of the springs." In her book by the same title, Trobish compares this maternal role to a rock in the middle of the stream of life that is flowing all around her. This book encourages mothers to create an environment of emotional comfort and a legacy for their children and grandchildren. For years, I have been collecting material on this subject; in fact , my filing cabinet is filled with articles and ideas on children, having a nurturing home, and being a wonderful wife.

What happens to all of those dreams and desires? What happens to our high calling as "keepers of the springs"? Water that does not flow becomes stagnant. There are springs in me that must flow or they will become stagnant. And so are the streams of life within you that long to flow into the family that you have longed for. As singles, I believe we can take that same calling that God has placed within each of us and channel it towards something other than marriage.

Spiritual Motherhood, Part One

I have been extremely blessed with my own natural mother, Irene Brown. Truly she has fulfilled the role of keeper of the springs in our family. She has nurtured my sisters and me, prayed for us, and loved us unconditionally. The older I become, the more I realize how exceptional

Mother is. Many of my friends have grown up in homes that were like fast-moving streams without an anchoring rock.

In addition, other women have influenced me. In high school, for example, some college girls in my church initiated friendships with me, and made time for prayer and listening. All along my path have been wonderful relationships that God has used to influence me in many ways. Both before and after my college years, hours of prayer and Bible study with my pastor's wife helped to shape my values and life goals. Even in her very busy schedule "Sister Wrae," as we affectionately called her, always made me feel welcome and a part of her life. She was firm— "Don't be late for prayer, Angela"—but filled with love and grace for me. Most of all, she imparted to me a vision of a big God. Hearing her weep over people and nations made me want to pray along with her, "Lord, break my heart with the things that break Your heart."

During a particularly hard day of homesickness my first year away at school, I was missing my mother terribly. All at once I felt the big, soft, maternal embrace of Joyce Conner, my dean of women and assigned counselor, who had sensed that I needed a hug. It was as if God were smiling on me. This lady represented everything I ever wanted to be as a woman, and I will always be grateful for my long conversations with her. Though a spiritual giant in my eyes she also loved to laugh which is such an important part of these spiritual mother-daughter relationships.

Joyce Connor's sense of humor was also the reason I avoided getting into serious trouble at this Christian college. One afternoon, two of my friends called me with the hilarious idea to sneak into a men's dorm (where no girls were allowed at any time) and put itching powder in the guys' sheets. It went over even better that we had planned until somehow the victims found out who had done it. Up to that point, the whole thing had just seemed like a great prank to me; I hadn't really even thought about the serious violation of the rules. When I realized I was about to be in big trouble I called Dean Conner, sobbing about how sorry I was (especially since one of the victims happened to be her son). I later learned that she could barely keep from bursting into fits of laughter at the other end of the phone. She certainly did not condone my breaking the rules, but her firmness was warmly blended with love, grace, and humor. Her propensity to laugh freely made a marked impression on me, for joy is such an important part of our mentoring relationships.

If you are without older women mentors in your life, ask the Lord to bring one to you. Also, get to know some of the great mothers of the faith through reading Christian biographies and books by godly contemporary women authors.

Spiritual Motherhood, Part Two

I have always dreamed of having five children, not 2.5 but five. When my sister, Sunnie, and her husband, Shane, announced they were expecting my first niece, Caroline, I was overjoyed. Yet I had to deal with a sharp unspoken pain in my heart: I was not married, and I was not the one having a baby. I faced the same tenderness three years later when Shawn and Brian announced that Lydia was on the way. Why do I still have such a desire for children without the fulfillment of this desire?

As women, we were made to be mothers. Who can deny that physically we were created to receive life where it was to be nurtured for nine months, and then to give life through pain and take care of that life who was entrusted to us? I have what we labor-and-delivery nurses sometimes refer to as an "adequate pelvis." Laymen call it "wide hips." Twice in my life, each time over a broken heart, I have actually been described as "skinny." On both of these occasions, however, my adequate pelvis has remained, and I have taken comfort in the fact that at least one day it would be easy for me to have children. But here I am. Did God give me wide hips in vain?

The struggle of disappointment in an unfulfilled God-given desire presents a choice to die emotionally or to cling to Him lest you die. In the area of motherhood, I have had to ask for grace to surrender my *whys*, to trust without knowing why He appears to have withheld this good thing from me, to plant my feet upon the truth of His sovereignty, and not be pushed around by emotions. Deep in my heart of hearts, I know the Lord loves me. He knows my thoughts. He is aware of my longings, as they are part of who He made. And I can say, "Great is His faithfulness."

One woman that has greatly helped shape my life is Corrie Ten Boom. She had her young heart broken by someone she loved, yet she knew the Lord had closed that door to marriage. She never gave birth to a child, but she saw the rebirth of many. The springs of our lives can flow into the lives of others. Whether we have a house full of children or not, we can be nurturers. As someone who has had both a wonderful natural mother and some enriching spiritual mothers, I can hear the Lord saying to me, "Freely, you have received, Angela; freely give." I know that one way in which I can be a keeper of the springs as a single woman is to be a spiritual mother myself. May my heart's answer to the Father's call be: "Yes, Lord! Bring me spiritual babies and children. Let me pour my time into them instead of into that which is useless."

Not all of us will know the joy that follows labor pains, but we can all know the joy that follows eternal ones. Spiritual labor pains will also be painful, inconvenient, and overwhelming. As a mother pushes through the stage where she may scream out, "I can't take it anymore!" so spiritual mothers may endure the tough times knowing that the transformed life of a child is worth the effort. As a mother holds her new infant in breathless amazement, we also can be filled with wonder as we see new life in our spiritual children. We too can celebrate Mother's Day each May.

I am the proud auntie of two wonderful little girls. We have more on the way, but I don't know what their chromosome order is at present. Though they both have parents who love them dearly and strong Christian homes, I take my role in their lives seriously: to love them, pray for them, and enjoy their blooming personalities. If you have nieces and nephews, I would encourage you to be a part of their lives and prayerfully ask the Lord for creative ways to bless your relationships.

I am not the queen of wisdom when it comes to this role of being the model aunt, but I can share things that I have done. First of all, I carry their pictures in my Bible as a daily reminder of my responsibility to lift them up to the Lord; I want them to grow up knowing that I am praying for them. Also, I attend their dedications with as much devotion as I would attend their weddings.

I deliberately do not attempt to show them how much I love them by my gifts, though a highlight for me was an impromptu shopping venture at a Laura Ashley sale. I bought and shipped to Caroline a little dress covered in flowers complete with a hat and purse. I still have the recording of her ecstatic phone message when she received her gift a few days later. I will do the same for Lydia when she gets a little older. We have started a special doll tradition. I have enjoyed it as much as they have. When Caroline hit that four-year-old nurturing stage, I began the quest for the perfect lifelike baby doll and was completely thrilled to send it to her. That special phone message of her delighted squeals also remains in the archives. Another activity that I'm working on is a collection of scrapbook memoirs and pictures of them that is a great deal of fun as well. They are not my children but they are very special little people with whom I want to have special moments.

When Caroline is a little older, I want to introduce her to *Anne of Green Gables* and let that be a special event. Lydia, too, and all the other future little girls in our family. I have asked for special permission to accompany Caroline on her first airplane trip. The thought of being up in the clouds with that imaginative child makes me smile in anticipation. I want to teach my nieces and nephews to love the sound of rain, the feel of dew on bare feet; to throw rocks in the creek and watch the ripples, and to throw leaves on one side of the bridge and race to the other side to see them float downstream. Last fall, Caroline and I gathered beautiful leaves and ironed them between wax paper. When she was at my house recently, she exclaimed, "Sissy! You have our leaves on your refrigerator!" It doesn't take big things to make an impression on them, just little acts of love.

Nieces and nephews are not our only chance to practice spiritual motherhood. We are surrounded by motherless children. They have a biological mother somewhere, but are without the security of a mother's love. The eternal impact that we could have on someone's life is bigger than any mere words I could ever communicate to you. You may be called to go overseas like Amy Carmichael, who left her native Ireland home to spend the rest of her days rescuing thousands of babies and young girls in India from temple prostitution. She started the Dohnavur Fellowship that has been active more than ninety years and continues to provide shelter and spiritual care to homeless girls.

You may simply have to open your front door and offer lemonade to young girls in your apartment complex. You are pouring your life into something; if that something is not another person, I am afraid it might be yourself. If so, your streams are stagnant and lifeless.

I feel a need to pray for children and parents I see in public, and I always try to acknowledge them. Whenever there is an opportunity to touch a life, please do it. Release the stream of life within you, and allow those fresh waters to flow around you. Look at children with new eyes. Smile at them, and hug them when you can. But be aware: just as natural offspring can be a handful, so the spiritual variety can wear you out!

Joy and Pain of Motherhood

Recently, while boarding a plane for a ten-hour flight, I was thankful to see I had a seat at the bulkhead. For people with long legs, that is a nice place to sit. There was a congenial-looking Asian man at the end of the row with three empty seats between us. We acknowledged each other's presence, and he seemed to frown while nodding toward the toys scattered on the floor between us. I got comfortably settled but decided not to take off my hiking boots, as I had been wearing my thermal socks for two days and there was hardly anything of a feminine nature about them.

The bathroom door opened and out walked a young girl who looked like she had been through a car wash without her car. She had a whining three-year-old little girl at her side and what appeared to be a six-month-old boy on her hip. The baby had nothing but a diaper on and was obviously having diarrhea. These were to be my traveling companions for the next ten hours. I smiled weakly and asked if there were anything I could do to help her.

Without hesitating, she thrust the baby into my hands. I say "hands" because I held him in the air until I managed to get a magazine onto my lap. He was dripping diarrhea. I am not exaggerating; I can still remember what that little guy smelled like. He grinned up at me and settled back on my chest. I decided my socks could not be any worse than what was in my lap, so I pulled off my boots to enjoy the ride. She asked me to do everything but breastfeed the baby, and I did. It was that three-year-old girl I was ready to eject from the emergency chute. This child was a living terror, and I did not pass the test of patience. I did not pray for her; I only prayed that I would survive. I am not proud to say I stuck my tongue out at her when her mother was sleeping.

At another time, I was in a frame shop. A young girl approached me who looked like someone Charles Manson would date. She had spiked hair in three colors, a black leather vest, several silver chains to match her silver nose ring, and black eye shadow and nail polish. She hardly appeared to be someone who would have similar taste to mine in decorating, but she looked at me and said, "Hi, may I help you?" Her words did not surprise me, but the sweet wistful voice that came out of that mouth etched in black lip liner was hardly what I expected. I felt like a hypocritical Pharisee for the judgment I had felt toward her. The Lord spoke to my heart saying, "There is a little girl behind that black leather vest and I want you to show her My love." We talked for a while and actually she was a wonderful help in selecting colors for my framing project. I went back to see her, and she was not in. But I plan on seeing her again. May the Lord give us eyes to see into the hearts and lives of those who need His love, those who may need a little mothering.

As you open your hearts to children, be aware that the joys may be accompanied with maternal heartaches. One summer I worked in a home for orphans and troubled youth. One teenage boy, in particular, became very dear to me. Full of life and love, he longed to be loved by his parents. He would come into the kitchen and talk for hours with me while I peeled and chopped vegetables. When he ran away from our home to find his parents, I was deeply saddened. While out shopping one day, I saw him and ran to him, expecting that familiar hug of his. When he turned away from me, I had the sensation that my stomach had been violently kicked. Tears were blinding me as I made my way to the car. Do I regret the love and prayers I invested in his life? Not in the least. No loving mother, not even a hurt one, would. I just pray that the seeds I sowed in him have finally found root in his tender heart and that someone else loved him along the way.

If you are willing to invite children into your life, opportunities to do so are endless: support a child or two in another country, join a literacy program and teach a child to read, invite kids in your neighborhood to Vacation Bible School.

Crisis pregnancy centers and street ministries also provide avenues for us would-be spiritual mothers. I value the opportunity I had for one pregnant teenager to live with me for a short period of time. Pointing a frightened, unwed woman towards Jesus is both humbling and rewarding. There is a joy beyond words to hold a child who has been rescued from abortion and a pain beyond words to hold the shaking shoulders of a girl who is enshrouded with post-abortion grief or the guilt of prostitution.

There have been girls in my life that I am so grateful to have had the chance to invest in: to hear their hearts and pray with them, to hug them when they are hysterical, and to cry along beside them. The letters and wonderful memories will last a lifetime. Yes, there has been money spent on *their* weddings and baby presents, gifts bought with joy at seeing God answer our prayers. Now I want to know their children, love them, and be a part of their lives.

Let me encourage you to plant seeds of life in all the young, fertile hearts and minds that you can. And perhaps it will be the streams that flow from you that will water seeds planted already in those you meet. Let young lives sprinkle your life with freshness. And if you get stuck on a plane with a three-year-old terror, be kind and gracious. I have a strong suspicion that the Lord is going to give me another opportunity to live what I am saying.

Sister Friends

I've dreamed of meeting her all my life...a bosom friend—an intimate friend, you know a really kindred spirit to whom I can confide my inmost soul.

—Anne of Green of Green Gables

The streams from our heart will naturally flow beyond children and our homes and into the kindred spirits of our friendships, as Anne spoke about. These relationships play an important part of our lives, as a fresh water source, keeping us fluid with warmth, kindness, and laughter. Just as a full and forceful stream will turn into a trickle if not refurbished with fresh water, so our streams from within can become shallow and lifeless if they only give without receiving. I can write freely about friendships, not necessarily because I am always such an outstanding friend, but because my life has been filled with so many wonderful ones. I am thankful for the friends who have stood the test of hormonal upheavals, male crisis, bouts of insanity, and poor judgment. These friends show their love unconditionally on the days that I am blinded by my own imperfections. They speak words of life into mine as stated in Proverbs 15:23: "A word spoken in due season is like apples of gold in settings of silver."

Terry Meeuwsen writes heartwarming thoughts that so poignantly describe the essence of friendship in her book *Just Between Friends.* "A friend is one with whom you can pour out all the contents of your heart, chaff and grain together, knowing that the gentlest of hands will sift throughout it all, keep what is worth keeping, and with a breath of kindness, blow the rest away."

Faces of many such friends filtrate through my mind and invoke pleasant memories, indeed. Madeline L'Engle and Luci Shaw share a friendship of twenty-five years. They have nurtured it through much diversity and over a distance of three thousand miles. They talk about what they call "authentic friendships," those that reach out and give rather than always taking. This is a characteristic of my close friends;

the ones that have my best interest in mind and are focused on giving rather than receiving.

Their relationship prompted me to think of my friendships over the long years. Though I haven't yet celebrated twenty-five years of a close friendship with anyone outside of my sisters, I look forward to long journeys with many. Of all the many rich and wonderful blessings in my life, it is my friendships that I count as one of the dearest treasures.

My earliest memories of friendships began from those slumber parties with giggling girlfriends. On more than one occasion, I ran to the bathroom with laughter-induced bladder spasms, and as an adult, I have sometimes wished I were wearing a protective undergarment. The splashes of laughter and joy in friendships are not to be counted as unspiritual. Many Scripture verses affirm laughter and joy. Proverbs 17:22 says "A cheerful heart is good medicine, but a crushed spirit dries up the bones." Certainly meaningful friendships are filled with more than moments of hilarity, but laughter is so important in keeping our hearts and spirits alive.

In addition to the warmth and joy that we know in our friendships, we should be particularly devoted to two areas that promote a Christ-centered relationship. As a keeper of the springs with our sisters, we can know a deeper flow of fellowship through prayer and accountability. Some of my richest times in friendships have been as we have shared our lives in prayer. For most of my life, I have always had at least one friend that I prayed with regularly. We try to meet together at a specific time every week or at least on the phone. Moments of prayer are a wonderful eternal investment for friends to make together. We pray for one another, but also for the multitude of needs around the world and us. If you have never prayed regularly with a friend, I would strongly encourage you to take advantage of an opportunity. Make yourself available. Let the Lord guide you and use you to encourage each other in your daily spiritual walks.

Faithful Friends

The Bible speaks of the faithfulness of friends in what I believe is the context of addressing blind spots in honest and kindness. "Iron sharpens iron; so a man sharpens the countenance of his friend" (Prov. 27:17). If we are wise, we will welcome those friends who can be counted as faithful to have the courage to speak the truth into our lives. It takes a strong foundation of trust and commitment to have that honesty. However, if truth cannot be spoken in love and without judgment, it should not be given. These sometimes sensitive issues should always be covered in prayer while asking for wisdom.

One of my very closest friends was spending a great deal of time with a man when she was at a very vulnerable time in her life. I was uneasy and concerned for her, yet I hesitated to verbalize my concerns. Later when she told me she was pregnant, I shed many tears of regret that I had not spoken the truth to her in love. Oh, that I had not only been sensitive but obedient. On one occasion in my life when I was "blinded by love" a couple of my male friends intervened and helped me to see things clearly. Male friends who are willing to face a hysterical female are true friends!

As seasons change in our individual lives, so also our friendships may assume a different dimension. When close friends marry, there will inevitably be changes in your relationship. They no longer have the freedom to spontaneously go out for coffee, to the beach or a weekend trip away, or sometimes even to pray together. It usually means no more late-night conversations—now *that* is the tough one! Be careful that you understand the new role of your friend and are willing to bend to her new life. And when the children come, embrace the opportunity that they provide as an endearing extension of your friendship. Be a part of their young lives so they know who you are. And if you start to feel like their mother doesn't have time for you, it's probably because she doesn't! Sometimes she doesn't even have time to go to the bathroom.

Be thoughtful and creative in keeping your friendship going. I love having pictures of my friends' children in my home. Although I don't make all their birthday parties, I do try to go to recitals and dedications with an occasional baseball or soccer game. The last softball game I attended, I found myself yelling like one of those out-of-control moms! As keepers of the springs, the relationships with our friends' children will always be a current of refreshing life.

Though friendships are usually warm and easy flowing, occasionally you may have to tread rough waters. At times a relationship can subtly become life draining if someone is clinging to you rather than to the Lord. The springs of your friendship will become dry and parched. You may need to gently draw boundaries. Point your friend to the Lord, for He is the only one that can feel that inner longing for which she is looking. Commit the friendship to the Lord for His safekeeping and pray for her. Most likely there will be pain in the transition, but let it be sprinkled with grace, mercy, and love. On the occasions where forgiveness is needed, given, or asked for, remember those moments are part of the strength of your friendship. Streams of water sometimes flow quietly and soothingly and at times there are some rocky white waters. These are all part of the streams of our lives and should be embraced.

C.S. Lewis shared his thoughts on friendship in many of his writings and particularly in *The Four Loves*. He felt that friendship is the greatest of worldly goods. He points out that friends don't spend time face to face and gazing into one another's eyes as someone in love does. They share common interests, goals, tenderness, and affection toward one another. And above all, they look together to a common Lord. If the direction in a friendship gets a little awry, be liberal in grace for one another. A friend of mine in a very dark period of her life pulled away in isolation and offended several of our friends with her silence. Not knowing what else to do besides pray, I sent her flowers with a simple, "I love you. I am here when you are ready." She shared with me later that though she was not in a place where she wanted to talk, the simple beauty of the flowers and my acceptance kept the door of her heart open until she was ready to share. Many years later, our friendship is one that I cherish deeply. Let us be careful not to get easily offended if a friend doesn't respond as we feel she should. She may not need your words but only your quiet love, your faithful friendship.

Faces of Friends

Of the many rich expressions of my friendships that I love, I find their diversity one of my greatest enjoyments. My friends are a smorgasbord of personalities and backgrounds; all are wonderfully different, but each makes up an important part of my life. Through the years, I have developed close relationships with some outwardly polar opposites. For example, I met my neighbor after going through her trash pile. I had spotted a darling little table that I knew would be a wonderful recipe holder.

People who throw away furniture tend to be most different from those who pick it up on the side of the road. And we are no exception. She is an engineer who thrives on structure and order, while the only thing structured in me is my molecular make-up. After seeing what a little sanding and polyurethane had done to her discarded table, she asked if I could help her with her decorating. In assessing her home, I commented, "There is not *one* thing in here that is not symmetrical." She's a two-candlesticks-with-flowers-in-the-middle kind of girl. Her kitchen cabinets display cans in perfect order, vegetables grouped together in their respective families from small to large. She doesn't need to change her style, just add some warmth: books, flowers, color, and perhaps a little bit of deviation from symmetry. Of course, I could use some of her order! We have a full and vibrant friendship, but if I ever married someone like her, he or I would have to have a lobotomy.

Another detailed, structured, and somewhat opposite friend, Candyce, kindly opened her home to me for a supposed transitional three-month period in my life. Two-and-a-half years later I moved out. During that time, we only entertained together once. A few friends over for stir-fry and homemade ice cream turned into about thirty-five guests in a small two-bedroom condominium without a yard. It was mass chaos, so of course I considered our dinner party a great success. I tided up hurriedly before the company arrived and stored some items in the bathtub: my Nordic chair, computer, several paper bags of projects, and the remains of a yard sale. Unfortunately, because of our limited space we had also decided to make the homemade ice cream in the bathroom. When one of the guys went into the bathroom to start the ice cream, he peeked behind the shower curtain and called all the guests in to see his discovery.

Honestly, you would have thought they had found a dead body or something. Candyce wasn't laughing about my having tarnished her well-deserved reputation as a neat housekeeper. Some years later, she and I got together for breakfast a few weeks before her wedding. Feeling emotional and nostalgic, I told her how much I had appreciated our time as roommates, knowing my out-of-the-line living had been challenging for her at times. I expected a sweet and gracious reply like, "Oh, Angela, it was wonderful rooming with you." Instead, she smiled and replied, "Oh Angela, I'm sure living with you helped prepare me for marriage."

"Oh."

In truth, I knew she was right, and in my heart of hearts I was glad to have finally helped her with *something*. Candyce, a graphic artist, is the epitome of order and organization, and I always felt like our relationship was a little lopsided in the area of practical service to one another. She seemed to serve me a lot, particularly in her inspiration to orderliness, for I needed all the help I could get. But I didn't feel like I could do much for her, other than lend an occasional listening ear, boost her spirits by making her laugh, and pray with her on a regular basis.

Like Candyce (and unlike me), my friend Stephanie also has the gift of organization. She has used this talent to help me. A year and a half ago, she spent three days at my house reorganizing my filing cabinet and setting up a system that is easy to maintain. At my request, she also blitzed through my closets and drawers and bagged up everything I no longer wore. She was not the least bit concerned about my emotional attachments to these items, ignoring my screams and laughing at my pitiful whines. I didn't mind her seeing all the disarray because I knew she loved and accepted me, disorganized filing cabinets and all.

Sometimes the diversity of a friend touches a place in the center of our souls that we would never expect. During an April evening a couple of years ago, I was tired yet content from an afternoon spring fling in the yard with my newly planted flowers. Sorting through the mail I found a small package from my friend Ruth with an enclosed tape. She and I, are without an doubt, incongruously *diverse*. If you were to compare us to flowers, she is a "delicate, tender *eidle wies*," and I am a "loud, flaming red hibiscus." But let me tell you, that *eidle wies* friend of mine emanates a most lovely and captivating fragrance.

Ruth is an accomplished musician and college professor of piano. She had composed a selection of songs she had recorded for me. As her voice filled the quietness of that April evening, I unexpectedly began to sob uncontrollably as I listened to the words of the first song, "Waiting for Him." She tenderly sang of a young woman who was waiting on the Lord first in her heart, though hoping for the day her husband would come. In a very faraway place in my heart, the Holy Spirit opened a window to my soul. It began to dawn on me that not only had she written that song for me but also it was about me. There were many, many tears of gratefulness that night as I listened to His voice through Ruth's music accompanied by her husband Scott. I had never had a song written especially for me and was humbled beyond anything I could describe. As exemplified in our friendship, Jesus has a way of taking diversity, blending it all together in His heart, and adding the flavor back into our lives.

Men Friends

The springs in our lives can flow into our friendships with males. Men play a different, yet important role in our lives. Some single women feel they can't maintain close friendships with males as they get older, but *thankfully* that is not true for me. The pure, affirming male friendships that I have in my life are some of my most cherished treasures.

My male friends have been vital in taking over in areas that I had no desire being a part of. An example that comes to mind is an event that I had to participate in because it took place in my home. Leaning on the kitchen counter in the mid-morning, I watched the slow drip, drip, drip, of coffee. I had gotten in late the night before from an international trip and was at a severe caffeine deficit. The aroma of the substance was wonderful. I poured my first cup and began savor the moment of that first morning swallow.

Suddenly I had the strangest sensation that I was not alone. I heard a slight hissing from beneath my kitchen cabinet and thought it was a leaking water pipe. Innocently I opened the door to find myself staring into the eyes of the biggest possum I had ever seen. She was huge and really ugly (as if I have ever seen a cute one), and blatantly was hissing at me like she was a wild animal or something. Complete pandemonium broke loose as I slung coffee and ran to my living room doing what any normal female would do. People have been arrested for disturbing the peace for less noise than I was making. The possum saga turned into what could be another book. I named her Priscilla the Possum. While I had been overseas for two weeks, Priscilla had made her way under my sink behind my dishwasher, and given birth to four baby possums.

In the middle of my crisis in the living room, my friends Barney and Victor called to check on me after my trip. Not able to understand what I was saying but hearing the hysteria in my voice, they were at my place in less than five minutes. Victor, who is from Africa and had never seen or heard of a possum, was especially chivalrous. As he entered the house with broom and garbage can lid in hand, he boldly declared, "I have come to slay the animal." At first sight of Priscilla, he jumped onto the kitchen stool and began his panicked African jungle calls. The two guys worked hard in my jungle kitchen for a couple of hours. Finally they had chased out Priscilla, but could not reach her babies.

After lying in bed that night and hearing her determinedly scratching to get in, I called my friend Scott and asked him either to come shoot her or shoot me. Several guys formed what I called the Homewood Possum Squad and hung with me till the bitter end. They tried to make me feel better by saying to me: "Of course she would choose your home, Angela. You're nurturing. You're hospitable. You're an obstetrical nurse. She is a smart possum." And I suppose she thought I might assist in her lactation needs as well? It took three weeks of ammonia, traps, and kicking on my cabinet doors to rid my home of those wretched creatures, and I was more than grateful for my wonderful male rescuers. When another friend, Bart, brought his utility vacuum to clean out her nest we found four jars of Gerber baby food. I now have a sign in my backyard that says "No Possums Allowed". But I admit, every time I see one on the side of the road, I smile.

A few weeks after my failed Bed and Breakfast venture, I detected a terrible odor coming from under my house. If I had learned anything from Priscilla, it was not to treat strange smells and sounds as if they'd just go away. I discussed it with a friend, and she suggested I call the police, as there was a missing homeless man in the news. "Perhaps he is under your house," she gasped. At that point I could believe just about anything, so I called. The Homewood police came to assess the situation. I stayed inside and wondered if I should go and get my hair cut since I might be on the evening news. They walked around and sniffed. "Yes Ma'am, it smells bad all right. But it's *no body* here," said one of the officers and laughed at his own joke. They said it was probably a dog and to call the sanitation department, which I did. So a couple of men from the sanitation department came by and sniffed.

"Yep, it smells awful all right," they said.

"Well, aren't you going to help me find out what it is?" I asked.

"Nope." Came their answer

"Well, could you at least help get my raked leaves onto your truck while you are here?" I pleaded.

"Nope. Do that on Tuesday. Today's Wednesday," they answered gruffly.

Muttering that I would like to stuff their bodies somewhere, I went inside to call a good friend. When I asked Charles, an international student who is always ready to lend a hand and earn tuition money, if he would like to make fifty easy dollars, he was over in a few minutes. I explained that I needed him to go under my house through the crawl space and see if he could find the source of the odor. Reluctantly, he agreed. "I just saw a documentary about killer bats," he said, his voice trailing off in uncertainty. "Would it make you feel better if I went with you?" I asked. His worried Malaysian face brightened up as he eagerly accepted my offer.

He went first, and I followed him on my hands and knees. Charles is much smaller in stature than I, so he easily fit through that little trap door. For me, it was like reliving my birth experience. After making it through with all parts intact, we crawled around in dirt and cobwebs, shining a flashlight without knowing whom or what we were going to find. *There are women who have made lots of money doing things like this with Harrison Ford* I thought, as my rear kept catching onto nails from the ceiling. We didn't find buried treasures or bodies: just one dehydrated rat that didn't even smell bad. It remains one of those unsolved mysteries. We ended our journey into the unknown, and I crawled out first, not because Charles was chivalrous, but because he had to push my rear end with his feet to help get me through a rather tight fit.

A Woman's Home

A guest is an adornment to a home.

—Uzbek proverb

As our springs of life flow through the role of motherhood and our friendships, they can also flow into our homes. Hospitality provides a wonderful channel for our natural creativity and homemaking inclinations. "Whoa," you may be thinking. "I don't subscribe to Martha Stewart's magazine, and I don't do hospitality unless I am invited." Fear not: long before dear Martha became so popular, the concept of hospitality was spoken of in Scripture as a godly characteristic. As early as Abraham and Sarah, the Old Testament gives us the example of serving meals and hosting guests. The New Testament reiterates the importance of hospitality. For example, the apostle Paul wrote, "Share with God's people who are in need; practice hospitality." I am very blessed to have a mother who has always taken these scriptural admonitions to heart. Growing up, I saw firsthand the joy and life given and received by

Mother as she opened her heart and home to the countless people who crossed our threshold.

We women are homemakers whether we are married or not. And we should take advantage of the opportunity to have both single and married friends into our homes. Ask yourself: "Whom can I reach out to?" "Who needs to be encouraged?" or "Whom would I like to get to know better?" Don't let a modest apartment, limited facilities, or poor cooking skills keep you from opening your home to the people God is placing in your path. If you get caught up in the performance of entertaining, you may end up as a hyperventilating hostess. But if you serve from the heart, you will find endless imaginative and fun opportunities to let your streams of life flow into others.

When I was in high school, a large group of missionaries came through our church. My parents were in the process of adding on a large living area, and there was rough wood on the walls, pink fiberglass everywhere, and a cement floor—certainly not your dream environment for entertaining. But these conditions presented no obstacle for my creative Mother's hospitable spirit. She arranged huge serving tables with decorative tablecloths and put fresh flowers on each table, and a wonderful evening was had by all. I always recall that event when feeling stressed out about not having everything perfect for guests.

As in Mother's case, our homes are a reflection not only of our decorating style but also of our spirit. They should be sanctuaries and not just decorated houses. A few years ago this contrast became clear to me after I had stayed in both types of homes on consecutive evenings. My journal entry from the second night records my impressions: "*Tonight I lie in bed and write from a little home that would never win an award with* Home Beautiful, *yet it is a Beautiful Home, for the spirit of Christ rests and dwells here. What a different place from the decorator's dream house that I was in last night. I like this one better.*"

In defining the spirit of your home, be creative! Though your house does not have to look like a decorator's showplace, clean can be nice, especially in the bathroom and kitchen. If it really looks bad, you might consider pulling your circuit breaker, announcing that the electricity is out, and lighting a bunch of candles. Could be cozy. Fresh flowers are a must for me; I always try to keep some in my house, usually from my own yard, though admittedly at times from my neighbor's yard. Picking freely from the neighborhood hydrangeas after dark has been a real source of temptation for me.

Numerous trips overseas have afforded me the chance to be creative in hospitality. Several years ago I spent a couple of weeks with friends in a seven-dollar-a-day, cold-water-only hostel in Jerusalem. For our evening meals everyone contributed a few shekels for food, and I somehow got designated to do the cooking. That time in my life was when I really began to embrace the role of hostess. The cooking conditions were challenging, to say the least: no hot water, and utensils that we would never think of using in our homes. But like Mother, I knew imagination and a generous spirit were the keys to genuine hospitality. I picked up fresh flowers at the market and arranged them in a plastic Coke bottle wrapped in tissue paper with ribbon (the only vase I could create). It was gaudy but appropriate for the setting. We had wonderful times of conversation and fellowship around the dinner table every night. Our hearts were truly touched and blessed.

A few weeks later I became the hospitality coordinator for a prayer ministry on the Mount of Olives. For Thanksgiving I had aspirations to serve the classic holiday feast to our many American guests and other American friends living in Jerusalem. Because of the Middle Eastern markets in which I shopped, however, our meal was hardly typical. The only things close to what the Pilgrims ate were mashed potatoes and sweet potato pie. The circuit breaker kept blowing when I had more than one oven going, and I had to keep running to the Arab neighbors to use their ancient baking stone for my pies. I think they were totally entertained by the way the Americans celebrate Thanksgiving. The pure bedlam of my kitchen was softened with a great deal of laughter.

Those experiences in Israel taught me once and for all that I could do what I'd always seen my mother do. After overcoming the obstacles of cold water, antiquated utensils, and ancient cooking stones, I returned to the United States confident that nothing, not even a lack of space, could squelch true hospitality from the heart. Admittedly, I have gotten carried away a few times. On one occasion, for instance, I wanted to get to know a family from church, so I invited them, two parents and four children, to Sunday lunch. Since I was cooking anyway, I rationalized I would invite another family as well. Why not include a couple of the single girls? And what about Max, since he loves to eat my food? My intended Sunday lunch for six turned out to include sixty others! We set up a croquet set outside, where the guys played aggressively while sliding around in the mud and pouring rain. It was a wonderful afternoon filled with laughter. My friends now refer to that event as "Angela's intimate luncheon with the Nickersons."

I've learned that messes shouldn't keep me from entertaining, either. On more than one occasion, I have stashed the dirty pans in the refrigerator or hidden them in the oven as guests were walking in the door. Now I just stick to the fridge. The last time I put dirty pans in the oven, I forgot and turned it on; later I had to clean out what looked like a nuclear meltdown.

Once I was preparing a Christmas tea for about fifty women. Having been interrupted that morning, I was still cooking a few minutes before everyone arrived and had no time to wash the dishes. There wasn't a dishwasher in this home, so I opened up the back door and piled all my dirty dishes and pans on the back porch. Martha Stewart would probably have done the same thing without hired help. At another party, the kitchen sink erupted like a geyser. We took all the dirty dishes outside and washed them by candlelight. It was kind of romantic, though the guy who was helping me wash them ended up going out of my life like the dirty dishwater.

Sometimes my good intentions to open my home don't turn out exactly as I expected. After the unfortunate possum incident under my sink, I breathed a sigh of relief and was thankful to return to life as normal once again. Setting out new candles and dusting the fresh sheets with some romantic fragrance, I smiled in anticipation of a wonderful weekend. There were fresh flowers by the bed and a bottle of sparkling cider cooling in the fridge. My home was immaculate, and romantic music was playing in the background, but it wasn't for me. I slipped out the door and headed to a friend's house to spend the night.

For a long time, I had wanted to do something for my friend DeeDee, a girl to whom I had been a spiritual big sister during her teenage years. Now that my "Wild Kingdom" experience was over, I invited DeeDee and her husband, J.B., to use my home for their first year anniversary getaway. They were both still in college and on a budget, so it seemed like a creative and romantic idea for them. Little did I know the romantic ambiance would be shattered by the untimely hatching of fleas that Prissy and her possomettes had left behind. Instead of candles, I should have set out flea bombs. Thankfully, in true friendship DeeDee and J.B. appreciated my good intentions, though interestingly enough, they haven't yet been back to spend the night with me.

Friends, we have the opportunity to demonstrate to the world that limited facilities and minor annoyances cannot tame our hospitable spirit. Even if you don't have a place of your own, you can organize a cookout or a picnic. Progressive dinners are always great, and clubhouses are readily available. For one of my favorite parties, I set up tables outside on a wonderful autumn night. The tables were adorned with pretty cloths and candles stuck in old wine bottles that I had collected from a fraternity house. Fall mums were everywhere. And if I say so myself, a more charming place could not have been found!

What if you don't like to cook? No problem. There are so many easy recipes available, and you can certainly pick up ready-made things, if you can afford to spend the money. Even if you serve bologna sandwiches on white bread, throw a sprig of parsley to the side and everyone will assume bologna is now trendy. Once, I sent out pretty invitations for "an evening of fine conversation and dining." The guests arrived and my menu for the evening included homemade vegetable soup, cornbread, and iced tea. We sat on the front porch in the swing and rockers and had a wonderful, simple evening.

I drive my mother to the point of exasperation when she watches me cook, since I really make a mess and usually have too many things cooking at once. But it *usually* always turns out great and I truly cannot remember an irredeemable disaster. I remember a time the piecrust was too hard and it went flying across the room when my guest tried to cut it. It was a great opportunity for laughter! If the roast burns or the cake falls, you just have to see that your identity is not wrapped up in the success of a twelve-layer French torte. And neither is your hospitality!

Overflowing Springs

As we learn to be the keeper of springs for others and drink from the fountain of relationships God has given us, we will be touched to the very depths of our souls. Not long ago I thought that I had been touched to the deepest depths by my friends. From laughter to prayer to diversity and times of rescue, I could say with gratefulness "my cup runneth over." I didn't know, however, I would soon experience a greater portion of a "full cup." Soon I was to tangibly feel the love of friends that would bear my pain and embrace my cross as they carried it with me. This has forever and quietly humbled me.

One gray morning a few months ago, my mother called me with the most devastating news I had ever received: my father's malignancy had spread, and he had only been given a few days to live. As darkness swirled around me, I was aware that God had allowed my close friend Maureen to be there when I received the call. She held me and then prayed as she drove me to the hospital. Later that afternoon my friend Ginger came to my door with eyes of compassion, love, and a simple "what can I do?" She, Maureen, and I changed sheets and cleaned my house in preparation for my sisters and their families who were coming in from out of town.

In the darkness of that day and the ones following, a fortress of strength surrounded me from my wonderful friends. I had never faced such a mountain of fear and pain, yet never once did I feel as if I faced it alone. They were as a hedge of protection from the infiltration of overwhelming grief. No one offered answers—just dear, sweet, unconditional love. Through them I understood as never before what Jesus meant in John 15:13 when He said, "Greater love has no man than this: that he lay down his life for his friends."

As I lost count of cards, calls, gifts, and embraces, I couldn't help but be reminded of the many times I had meant to send a card or call someone who needed to hear my voice. I just never got around to it. How grateful I am that my friends and loved ones didn't put me on a list of things to do and forget about me. They entered into my circle of conflict and pain with compassionate hearts and tears as a deep reservoir of life.

A good keeper of the springs never forgets about those whom the Lord has given her to mother, host, or befriend. She is faithful to serve them in her role as a rock in the middle of the stream of life flowing all around her. As single women we have such abundant opportunities to flow into the lives of those who surround us. Drink freely of the living water that flows from your Father's hand so that you might spill over with life and refreshment to hearts that are dry and brittle. As you do so, you will know joy that floods your heart like a flowing river. And you will never be thirsty for life again, not even for a single moment.

Chapter Three

FEARFULLY AND
WONDERFULLY MADE

One spring night in Alabama when I was ten years old, I was on my knees praying my usual "God bless my family and everybody in the world." I then prayed for something especially important. "Lord Jesus, I know that you can heal people. And so, if you can make limbs longer, surely you can make them shorter. Would you please make my feet smaller? Amen." Concluding this time of deep intercession, I got up from my knees, sat on the edge of the bed, and swung my legs around. I felt blinding pain and heard a terrible noise. My feet had made contact with the fan blades. It took me a few moments to gather the courage to look down. This was not how I had intended for my prayer to be answered. All toes were intact, though, and as long as ever.

I am not exaggerating; my feet are longer than most men's. As a teenager, this presented a terrible problem, as the only shoe style for my size foot was the matronly kind. Fortunately, it is now easier to get fashionable shoes in my size. However, when I fly, I pack a change of clothes, my journal, and all my shoes in a carry-on. That way, if my luggage gets lost, I have all the irreplaceables with me. I have always said I wanted to marry someone with feet bigger than mine. Maybe that's why I am still single.

My big feet have not been my only complaint about my physical appearance. I have what I call the Renaissance Look. In a society that caters to Gap and Ann Taylor figures, this doesn't exactly promote wonderful feelings within. If I had lived before the twentieth century, I could have been a model for the perfect figure. Walking through the Philadelphia Museum of Art last summer, I spent a lot of time in the nineteenth century section with all the exquisite paintings of "plus size" women. They lie around by Roman pools eating grapes, wearing almost nothing, and appearing unconcerned about all that excess weight, while we feel compelled to camouflage even a few extra cells. I especially love Renoir's paintings. My favorite one is a portrait of his wife after the birth of their child. She has a sweet face and all of her post-partum left-overs as well. Renoir is said to have kept this endearing and personal portrait for himself. Perhaps there is another Renoir out there who will want to paint me.

Several years ago I became particularly sensitive about my weight. Though I didn't know it, I had a malignancy in my thyroid gland and was in a metabolic crisis. All I knew was that I was close to twenty-five pounds overweight and my scales, like the stock market, were going up every day. During one week at the height of this disorder, three people asked if I was pregnant. My level of self-acceptance was less than opti-mal, to say the least.

Ironically, during that same week I was giving my last medical pre-sentation for an abstinence program for inner-city high school boys. The leader of these classroom bullies had been extremely obnoxious, and I had warned him for the last time: the next outburst and he was on his way to the principal. As I was wrapping up the presentation on dating and AIDS, the bell rang and he yelled out, "You are too ugly to date and too fat to have AIDS." Trust me, I wasn't devastated by his assessment of me. Before the classroom emptied out, I managed to retort that I was not fat but *voluptuous* and that I knew that, in his ado-lescent way, he was just flirting with me.

Speaking of voluptuous, a toy maker's marketing directors recently made a decision that I found somewhat reassuring. Apparently, they have added some cellulite to a doll's otherwise perfect figure. She will have a little less in some places and a little more in others. What is bound to happen, of course, is that the little girls who play with her will want her to have plastic surgery just like their mommies. Plastic surgery, to alter the less-than-perfect figures that the rest of us seem to have, is becoming as common as being fitted for glasses. Which I suppose is not a bad thing if you are a plastic surgeon or you're married to one.

I met a mother at a little friend's tea party one week. This woman had the shapeliest legs I had ever seen; they seemed to go on forever, and she was wearing a skirt to show them off. I finally asked her whether she exercised hours a day or had had plastic surgery. She said her calves were in her genes and that her father had the same type of legs. It's funny; my legs are as long as hers but it is clear to me that we are not even remote cousins.

Obviously, like most women I am at times overly concerned about my looks. I particularly wanted to look good for my high school reunion, and evidently I succeeded. Throughout the evening, I was charmed by all the compliments I received. "Gosh, I just can't get over how good you look!" "Angela, is that really you? Wow! You look so nice!" Or "You just look marvelous!" Their flattery splashed me with joy. But when my name was announced at the end of the evening as "The Most Changed Female" along with my now bald-headed classmate as "The Most Changed Male," I didn't exactly know how to interpret it. I still don't.

The Apparent Image

Of course, we Christian women know in our heads that outward appearance is far less important than the condition of our hearts. Why then do we face the same struggle as our secular society when it comes to a preoccupation with image? Why are we so worried about how others see us? All of us sometimes fall into the trap of getting our identity from what we are on the outside. We might feel the labels we wear and what we drive project our self-image. If that is true, I am now projecting the image of a grandmother. Someone was gracious enough to give me a car that is nice and matronly looking. It fits my image about as much as black fishnet hose and a leather miniskirt. At least I used to get flirted with when I drove trendy cars.

The car before this one wasn't much better. It was a ten-year-old pea-green Mercedes station wagon. Since it had no power steering and the sunroof was a manual crank, it was kind of like driving around in my own private gym. I had the most well-defined biceps I had ever had, especially in my right arm, from cranking open the sunroof.

These cars have done wonders for me. Practical conversation pieces, they have served as constant reminders that my identity is based on the eternal work that God has done in my life rather than on temporal things. They have also taught me to laugh at myself. If I did not know how to laugh at myself, I am not sure what sort of twisted emotional state I would be in. Indeed, this ability to take myself lightly was responsible for my entering and winning a statewide speech contest in which I delivered a humorous talk about my big feet. Accepting ourselves as our Creator made us means we accept ourselves with all of our unique and quirky ways. I am not talking about embracing character flaws or weaknesses, but rather accepting the unique blend of our personality types.

There have still been times that I would like to be repoured back into the mold from which I came and physically change some things. But I often recall how I felt that spring night when I looked down and saw my toes intact. At that young age, I asked the Lord to help me to be grateful for the way He had designed me physically. But what about the uniqueness of my personality? Isn't that part of who He made me as well? I decided years ago that my naturally curly hair roots must be imbedded in my brain cells. Sometimes my life is just wild, kinky, and at times frizzy, though I have tried in vain to tame it. Regardless of my efforts, there seems to be no escape from my personality.

A few years ago, for example, I was in Utah for a few days of skiing. After a day at the slopes, I was visiting with a friend who was having a home fellowship. There was no time for a shower, so I thought I would at least wash my hair quickly in the bathroom sink. It would take two minutes max. As I prepared to rinse out the shampoo, I found my head was wedged between the faucet and the drain. If it had been my hips, I might have understood, but my head of all things is not unusually big.

I could not budge it even one centimeter. Fortunately, I had the sense to turn the water off so I wouldn't drown. I was really beginning to feel pain, as well as panic. No one could hear me screaming, since they were all upstairs. After working my chin back and forth for several minutes, I finally managed to dislodge myself. Meanwhile, my friend and his guests had begun to wonder what was taking me so long. When I finally arrived upstairs, I told them what had happened just because I was so grateful not to have been decapitated. This room full of people was howling though they had never met me. So much for my "together" image I had wanted to present, especially to the single guy my friend wanted me to meet! And so I joined their laughter. The next night I headed for the shower rather than the sink.

Another naturally curly sort of event occurred when I spent a week at Wheaton College for a writer's conference. During a break, I was taking a scenic and leisurely stroll across the lovely campus, where there happened to be a lot of construction going on by handsome, muscular men who nodded and seemed to wave. I was feeling rather cute that day so I smiled and proceeded down a sidewalk only to discover that I was wading in freshly laid and smoothed cement. I screamed and was afraid to move. The man who had labored so hard was looking at me disgustedly, and the rest were grinning. I apologized and asked if he would like me to autograph the cement, while it was still wet. He didn't appear amused. As I looked back, I could see my perfectly formed footprints. And at that moment I could envision the next morning's headlines in the campus paper: Miss Bigfoot arrives in Wheaton. While wiping the cement off my shoes I thought, *I came here to learn how to report, not to be reported about.*

Now, you have to understand these sorts of events occur on a regular basis for me, and have my entire life. I think it may have started when my mother dropped me head-first into the dishwater as an infant. She's never mentioned how long I stayed underwater. I have grown accustomed to the most unexpected mishaps and usually stay fairly calm in the midst of them, which usually contributes to a reasonable outcome.

For instance, while teaching a prenatal class to first-time expectant parents, I was demonstrating how to bathe a newborn infant—something all new parents are worried about. Assuring them that their precious baby would not break, I held the plastic doll in front of them and showed them how to secure the infant's neck while bathing the head. To my horror, the doll's head fell off and went rolling across the floor. There was silence as we all stared at the floor. Maintaining my composure, I walked over, picked up the poor baby's head, screwed it on, and calmly said, "Now that should never happen to you, but in the event that it does, make sure you put the baby's head back on facing the right direction." Instead of squirming in fear, they all laughed. And I did too.

It's easy to allow embarrassing situations to affect your self-image. After a string of unhappy events like these, you might even be tempted to begin thinking of yourself as clumsy or hopelessly inept. But in addition to diffusing awkward moments, laughing at yourself—with or without an audience—is one way to remind yourself that circumstances don't "define" you. And neither do people's impressions of you. Our true definition comes from God's love and work of grace within us. He created us and knows us inside and out.

More Than the Outward Appearance

Several years ago I came across some literature that helped me better understand and accept myself as a cherished and unique creation of God. While housesitting for some friends, I discovered a book on temperaments. Getting into bed that night, I settled in for some interesting reading. My interest soon turned to fascination. I found that I easily fit into one major temperament, Sanguine. But I was completely discouraged to find I was off the chart on the negative characteristics (impulsiveness, self-centeredness, and inattentiveness to detail...there were a lot more) with only a sprinkling of the positives (flexibility, optimism, and spontaneity). I flung the book to the other side of the bed and turned out the light. Later that week I finished the book and entered a new realm of self-acceptance and understanding of myself.

Another fellow Sanguine is Florence Littauer, author of *Personality*

Plus. She briefly describes the four temperaments as:
   *a spontaneous, vivacious, cheerful Sanguine
   *a thoughtful, faithful, persistent Melancholy
   *an adventurous, persuasive, confident Choleric
   *a friendly, patient, contented Phlegmatic

Learning about my personality type has proven very helpful to me, as it has taught me how to deal with my weaknesses more effectively and utilize my strengths more productively. Our personalities are the very essence of who we are. It was actually Hippocrates who introduced the four basic temperaments: Sanguine, Phlegmatic, Melancholy, and Choleric. Gary Smalley and John Trent have a delightful way of communicating the four temperaments through animals: the Otter, the Golden Retriever, the Beaver, and the Lion. At one of their seminars, I heard John Trent, a fellow Otter, explain how he had changed checking accounts because his account was beyond all hope of reconciliation; I was delighted to know that I wasn't the only person who had ever taken such drastic measures. At the close of the meeting, I still remember him smiling at me understandingly as he drove out of the parking lot. I was standing by my car, while AAA Locksmith Service was getting my keys out.

All my life I have struggled with the sanguine characteristic of being impulsive. In major decisions I have simply jumped. Just as I was about to crash, I would fumble around to find my parachute. In one impulsive disaster I hired a cocaine-addicted contractor to work on my home, without checking him out first. He stole from me and ruined my floors and walls. What upset me most was that I knew I had brought about this crisis myself by jumping into the transaction without first seeking counsel from my father. Dad was recovering from surgery at the time, and I didn't want to bother him. Of course, the problems that arose from my independent decisions ended up bothering him more than my asking him for advice ever could have.

I'm thankful to say that I learned from my real estate disaster. Acknowledging my sanguine weakness of impulsiveness has helped me learn to control it somewhat, especially by seeking the counsel of non-impulsive people. Over the last four years, in decisions related to home maintenance I have repeatedly consulted my dad. I also sought my parents' advice before taking a leave of absence to write full-time. Without them, I might have left my job before I could have afforded to do so. But thanks to their guidance and counsel, I waited until the right time.

Formerly an insane sanguine and now just a sanguine, I am here to offer hope to anyone who feels trapped instead of Spirit-controlled in her temperament. Let me encourage you to identify your own personality type, along with your strengths and weaknesses. Littauer writes that in understanding our temperaments we:

* know *what* we are made of.
* know *who* we really are.
* know *why* we react as we do.
* know our *strengths* and how to amplify them.
* know our *weaknesses* and how to overcome them.

You will find it a fascinating study and remember to have a sense of humor along the way.

Beverly LaHaye encourages us from her book, *The Spirit Controlled Woman*, "Enjoy the richness of those strengths in your temperament; then ask God to help to modify the weaknesses that you might become more Spirit-filled and Christ-like." LaHaye encourages us that as we desire a spirit-controlled temperament, the Holy Spirit can indeed strengthen our weaknesses. "His strength is made perfect in our weakness."

Here is to an enjoyable and unique journey, for there is only one *you!*

Accepting the Past

In addition to accepting and dealing with our God-given personalities, we must also accept, often without understanding, our pasts. For many people, this presents a difficult challenge, which sadly some are never able to meet. While I have been blessed to grow up in a loving, Christian home, I realize more all the time how rare this blessing is. Many have grown up in insecure, even cruel environments. Regardless of your background, however, the grace of God is able to free you from the hurts of yesterday. And He who made you knows everything you have been through and still desires to use you.

Having been raised with the strong biblical teaching of an excellent pastor, Joe Fowler, I heard this truth all my life. It gained new meaning for me during my college years, however, after I met Christina, a new Christian, at church. I had invited her to go to my parents' home with me one night after a late-evening event, completely unaware of the maturing that was about to take place in me.

Around 1:00 in the morning , I closed my eyes and turned onto my side, where I began drifting off to sleep. Just then I heard a quiet voice in my heart that spoke in a way that no other voice does. "Angela, Christina has been involved in homosexuality." My eyes popped open and my heart skipped a couple of beats. Rolling onto my back, I looked up at the ceiling as if to question what I had just heard. Then I looked at Christina who was sleeping beside me. I calculated that the doorway leading out of my bedroom was approximately eight feet away, almost a short enough distance for one flying leap. I gazed back up at the ceiling and said silently, "This is great, Lord, *just* great. Now, what am I supposed to do?" Feeling the need to go brush my teeth again or *something*, I was slowly and quietly making my way out of bed when my new friend spoke up, "Angela, there is something I need to tell you."

This hurting girl then began to reveal an ugly past. Sadly her home, unlike mine, had not been a place where she had felt safe and at rest. It was not a place where trust, love, and security had wrapped themselves around her heart. Christina's parents had both died when she was a little girl. Though the men among her new respectable guardians were active in church and civic affairs, they had shattered her world of innocence through child molestation, which had ultimately driven her to a lesbian lifestyle.

The night that Christina shared this secret past with me was an eye-opener for both of us. I became more aware of my own blessings, as well as of others' hurts. She became more aware of the love and healing power of the God to whom she had recently committed herself and for whom she had renounced lesbianism. There was still a tremendous amount of emotional healing that needed to take place in her. Because of the Lord's sweet voice to me earlier that evening, I understood why

61

she had a fortress around her heart, and I was able to love and pray for her accordingly. In time and with prayer, I watched as the walls around her heart slowly begin to crumble, revealing a lovely, feminine creature hidden behind masculine barriers. With the unconditional love of many and through the help of biblical counseling, Christina eventually reflected the beautiful woman she was. She is now happily married with four children.

There are not many guarantees in this life, but one is that you will experience pain through the failure and hurt of people around you. Not all of these experiences will be as traumatic as Christina's. No matter how great or small the injury, God will give us the grace and courage to deal with the things in our past that need to be dealt with. Sometimes it is difficult to face these things. They are buried in our hearts and may remain unseen for a season, but eventually they will surface in our thoughts, attitudes, and actions. As we yield them to a patient, loving, and compassionate Lord, He will make us whole.

Regardless of the wrongs done toward us, God will help us to forgive. We live in a world that does not teach us to forgive freely and fully as we ourselves have experienced forgiveness. Often we delay forgiveness because we think the other person will never understand how much he hurt us if we forgive him. Amazingly, we may even think that this person doesn't deserve to be forgiven. If that is the case, we must remind ourselves of the day we bowed our heart and knees before the cross and received what we did not deserve.

Sometimes we may hang onto pain or bitterness because we don't want to let go of a wound that has been a part of who we are for such a long time. Unforgiveness is especially quick to grow in the soil of our hearts. Its treacherous root system spreads rapidly as it is nourished on bitterness. In addition to affecting our personality, it also quickly chokes our emotional and spiritual life. Forgiveness is the only way to develop a healthy root system, which produces the healthy fruit of the Holy Spirit and restores perfect fellowship with Him. God alone can help us to forgive. His word offers such hope to us: "He has come to heal the brokenhearted and bind up their wounds" (Psalm 147:3). When we allow Him to do this, like Christina we can finally stop focusing on our past and leave it behind. You are then free to share completely from a whole heart.

I demonstrated this principle once to a group of children I was working with. I used a huge flowerpot to plant seeds and watch them grow from week to week. I explained that first we had to prepare the soil, which would be parallel to our hearts. There were roots, weeds, and other debris in this soil. As each child pulled something from the dirt, we identified an issue that it might represent: anger, bitterness, ungratefulness, and judgment, to name a few. We replaced the weeds with seeds. In a few weeks, beautiful, colorful zinnias filled the enormous flowerpot. Most of these children had emotionally unhealthy homes and circumstances, but they could grow up to become healthy, life-giving plants if they kept the soil of their hearts tender and fertile.

I have always discouraged what I call the *Belly Button Syndrome*: forever gazing inward in an attempt to "fix" ourselves. Preoccupation with self inevitably leads to consistent defeat and ultimately to self-destruction. Instead of nurturing problems from the past with bitterness and anger, be willing to face them, let them go, forgive, and receive healing and cleansing. It is in this way that we can experience emotional wholeness. As He sets us free, we are able to offer hope and compassion to others along the way.

Accepting the past presents one of life's greatest challenges. But I have found encouragement in learning to see how God can use even the wrongdoings of others for His good pleasure in our lives. Corrie ten Boom, who suffered much at the hands of others, spoke of this truth. A Christian Dutch woman who secretly gave shelter to Jews during World War II and consequently spent time in the German concentration camp of Ravensbruck, she wrote these words: "This is what the past is for: every experience God gives us, every person He puts into our lives is the perfect preparation for the future that only He can see." In every circumstance, though we may not understand it, we can be absolutely certain that He is (and was) in control.

Accepting the Present

Once we have accepted our personality types and pasts as instruments in the hands of a loving God who is molding us, we must go a step farther and accept our present circumstances. As with our pasts, some of us face greater daily difficulties than others: poor health, broken relationships, financial problems. And obviously, the level of difficulty for each of us can change from one day to the next.

Sometimes the problem may be grave by anyone's standards, as was the case with Madame Guyon. If anyone had reason to be depressed, she did. This sixteenth-century French countess exchanged a life of comfort and ease for a rat-infested prison cell for the sake of the gospel. Nonetheless, in these dire conditions she wrote of despair as a sin: "I entreat you, give no place to despondency. For despondency is not a gross temptation of the adversary but a refined one. Melancholy contracts and withers the heart and renders it unfit to receive His grace." Madame Guyon seems to be cautioning us against the attitude that says, "I deserve to feel this way. No one understands how I feel. This is unfair." As she tells us, if we open our hearts to despondency and depression, we close them to His grace.

I have never endured the hardships of this sixteenth-century Christian heroine. However, in some despondent times of life I have succumbed to the temptation of which she spoke. I have wailed and thrown myself dramatically onto the bed. "I just can't take anymore!" Some of my most beautiful pillowcases are forever stained with lipstick and mascara as a reminder of the frequency with which I have been known to give this little performance.

Several years ago I was going through a difficult time, which I could best describe as being in an "emotional rainstorm without an umbrella." I felt as if I was in a tunnel of darkness stumbling to find my way out. I recalled a tapestry that I had seen in the home of Corrie Ten Boom's family living room in Holland and how I had been drawn to its beauty at the time. In her storytelling before she died, she described that same tapestry and how it parallels with our lives. On one side were dark colors and gnarled threads and knots, but on the other was a beautiful finished image whose colors were radiant. It reminded me not to be dismayed by the darkness of some of the colors in my life and that on the other side of this tunnel I would be able to see the richness of the tapestry that was being formed in me.

For several months I had to cling to this word picture. Daily I had to seek a seemingly silent God, knowing that He was faithful, regardless of my feelings. I also began seeing a professional Christian counselor for the first time, though spiritual pride nearly kept me from doing so. He was instrumental in giving wise and biblical counsel as he guided me through the tunnel until I once again saw clearly.

I believe strongly in biblical counseling during dark times, but I have noticed that people are sometimes more willing to see a counselor than they are to seek the Lord. Don't miss an opportunity to draw close to Him. All the counseling in the world cannot replace a close encounter with the living God. If we will allow it to do so, pain has a way of drawing our hearts to Him. "I waited patiently for the Lord," the psalmist wrote, "and He inclined to me and heard my cry and put a new song in my mouth and a song of praise to my God" (Psalm 40:1). Those lonely and dismal times can create new chords of praise. Just as the Lord created life and beauty in the beginning from a world that was covered in darkness, He can create beauty in the darkness of your circumstances and a tapestry that is beyond compare.

After months of struggling, I began to see this beautiful tapestry in my own life on a trip to London, England. As I walked through the city, I stopped in Hyde Park to read and watch the different entertainers who are always there: jugglers, artists, guitarists, and singers. Finding a spot in the grass, I pulled out my Bible and began to read. I was deeply drawn to Psalm 139. This chapter so beautifully describes God's perfect knowledge of us and His delight in creating us. I read from the chapter for several minutes, absorbing the truth of the verses.

To my surprise and dismay, I heard that same voice that had told me about Christina now tell me to get up and read the chapter aloud. How could I politely and respectfully say to God, "You have got to be nuts"? After several minutes of an internal battle, I stood up feeling more foolish than I ever had in my entire life. Thinking that I needed an audience, I walked over to a couple of street people, told them I was about to do a public reading, and asked if I could pay them to be my audience. They were not interested. "Fine," I said, a bit miffed.

Taking my place on the sidewalk, I opened my mouth and began reading the wonderful words from Psalm 139. "Oh Lord, Thou hast searched me and known me. Thou dost know when I sit down and when I rise up. Thou dost scrutinize my path and my lying down, And art intimately acquainted with all of my ways..." An inebriated man was soon standing at my side. I was actually thrilled to have the company. Pretty soon there was a small crowd around me listening, and I had a true audience! As I read this wonderful psalm over and over, I realized there was something breaking in my heart at the powerful truth of these words. I could hardly speak for the emotion I felt, because I understood, as never before, my Father's plan for me and His sovereign control of my life. I can't help but smile in remembrance of this unusual event, yet I know that my attitude has never been the same toward my circumstances or myself since that interesting and wonderful afternoon.

Psalm 139 reminds us that He has known us from the beginning and He already knows our end. He knows the details of the times in between. He knows us intimately and is acquainted with all of our thoughts and ways. He knows and loves our uniqueness because He made us fearfully and wonderfully. In our own extraordinary way, we are a reflection of Him.

When we read His Word and spend time in His presence, we give ourselves opportunities to hear from the Lord. Our time with Him in devotion, quietness, prayer, and Bible study keeps us whole and attuned to His Holy Spirit. It strengthens us in the knowledge that He loves us, designed us, and placed us where we are. It will give us the confidence to accept and submit to His design and control over our circumstances and ourselves: past, present, and future.

Chapter Four

FEMININITY IN A
MS. GENERATION

Stuffing the remains of my apple core into my paper sack, I sat back to watch the ducks on the pond. I was in London, England, enjoying an afternoon picnic at a park. Noticing a nearby hospital I suddenly felt strangely drawn to it. It wasn't because I have a nursing background and felt a natural curiosity about British hospitals, but because I somehow found this one irresistible. After a few minutes of reflection, I strolled over to the hospital and walked in; unable to escape the feeling that there was a reason I should follow my inclination.

The familiar sterile odor of disinfectant greeted me. *Where to now?* I wondered. The hospital seemed strangely empty and I felt alone. Unsure about what to do next, I stepped into the elevator and pressed the button for the fifth floor—for no other reason than that was the floor I worked on in the United States. I wondered what awaited me. The doors opened, and I turned left and walked along an empty corridor with no nurses and no patients—only a quiet hospital hall with empty beds. Reaching the end of the corridor, I turned around, thinking I should have stayed in the park with the ducks.

At that moment, I noticed a pair of bare feet sticking out of a bed and walked towards the door. Upon knocking, I heard a male voice say "Come in." Once in the room, I faced a handsome man in his late twenties, sitting up reading a newspaper. Smiling at me inquisitively, he said, "Hello."

I replied. "My name is Angela, and I just happened to be walking down the hall. I'm a nurse from the United States, and I thought I would say hi."

He held out his hand to me and said, "I'm so glad you did. My name is John, and I haven't had any visitors today. I'm very glad you are here." In our conversation, I found John pleasant, kind, and gentle. He volunteered that he was recovering from surgery and was scheduled to go home the next day.

"And what kind of surgery did you have, John? If you don't mind my asking, that is."

"Oh, not in the least. I had a hysterectomy," he said.

"Oh," I replied, a little taken aback.

"Have you ever taken care of hysterectomy patients?" John asked.

"Well, yes, I have, but they have usually been females. In fact, they have all been females," I answered.

Despite my surprise at John's revelation, I suddenly understood why I was standing in that room on that day and not in the park.

"John, I want to tell you the story of how I really happened to be in this hospital." John listened intently. "May I tell you about the love of Someone who knows who you are and why you are here?" I asked.

As I did so, my new friend listened with great interest and then shared quietly and tearfully of a life marked by deep confusion and pain. I heard the heart cry of a young woman who was so confused about her identity that she had gone to incredible lengths searching for peace.

Although John's case is certainly extreme, I have nonetheless found that many Christian females today, both married and unmarried, also face an identity crisis of sorts. In her academy-award-winning role in "The Rainmaker," actress Katherine Hepburn desperately cries out, "I just want to love someone and for him to tell me who I am!" Her desire mirrors that of many women. But we would be foolish to allow Hollywood or *Cosmopolitan* magazine to define what it means to be a woman. Their attempts to liberate women and foist their values on us have only created greater chaos. And, believe it or not, this kind of chaos is even more destructive than the kind to which I devoted a full chapter in this book.

The feminist movement, which began only a generation ago and has had an enormous impact on our society—even among Christian women—appears to be an outgrowth of this very insecurity. Former National Organization of Women (NOW) national press secretary Amy Tracy, who converted to Christianity and now works for a Christian organization, comments in an article in *World* magazine that "there's so much brokenness among the women today. Through activism, they're responding to the pain in their lives. They know they have a need, but they don't have a concept of what it is to know Christ." Gloria Steinem, editor of *Ms.* magazine and one of the most influential feminists, describes her childhood and formative years in her book *The Revolution from Within: A Book of Self-Esteem.* She writes about her losses, and one can't help but notice that her desire to be liberated seems to be closely linked to a lack of fulfillment in her life.

NOW, which claims to have a half-million members, managed to attract only eight hundred to a four-day conference in 1999. Women seem to be discovering that NOW may, in fact, be doing them more harm than good. Carmen Pate, another former feminist, says, "Many of the women who bought the feminist lies for all those years are now paying the consequences." In any event, it's clear that NOW doesn't have the answers for those of us who are struggling with our femininity.

How many "N"s in Femininity?

Femininity encompasses much more than outward appearance; rather it is an attitude toward ourselves, our homes, and our relationships. Joyce Conner, my dean of women at Portland Bible College, once said; "Femininity is a part of God's nature expressed through a woman that cannot be expressed through a man." Author Jean Lush describes the balance of strength, honesty, mystery, and femininity as "The Feminine Mystique." She is not talking about luring men into a web of intrigue, but about really discovering who we are as women of God's design. Nationally known Christian psychologist Dr. James Dobson, in a radio interview with Mrs. Lush, added his own thoughts: "I think of mystique as a quiet, inner confidence. A woman who has mystique has a certain belief in her worth, in her position, in her personality, and in her relationships." For years I have tried to articulate what I thought femininity really was, and their insights have helped confirm my own beliefs that femininity comes from within and not from without.

I have struggled with this issue all my life, since my DNA molecule does not include a petite gene. My college journal entries include reminiscences about a group of students with whom I drove cross-country to California and then flew to Washington D.C. The girls on the trip all just happened to be petite, an attribute which I have always associated with femininity, and in every other respect flawless. I was painfully aware of our differences: my hair was wild and kinky when straight was in; I felt clumsy while they seemed dainty; my face was hormonally challenged; and although I can't remember about my weight that week, I'm sure I was not happy with it.

At four thousand feet above the earth, I wrote: "*I have to change my attitude of self-criticism to a more positive one. I so want to be feminine inwardly and outwardly. I can truly say this, even though I just dumped my supper all over my lap, much to everyone's amusement. While walking down the aisle to the bathroom to pick the rice off my clothes, I backed into two trays and dumped them all over the floor. Oh my.*" A few hours later in the hotel, I wrote, "*Tonight, while sitting by myself on the bench waiting for the others, I fell off and nearly busted my head open on the marble wall. I have just taken two aspirin and am going to bed.*"

On rare occasions I feel as if I have the aura of Grace Kelly and the intrigue of Ingrid Bergman. I can smile alluringly as I sip my latte and inhale life. Those are pleasant but fleeting moments, however. For my birthday one year, I spent a pleasant evening with a male friend. Though our relationship was not romantic in any way, I felt wonderfully affirmed and delighted by his attention and compliments. At one point he told me something no one had ever said to me before: that I was cute when I wrinkled my nose. I thought only petite girls wrinkled their noses and had never been conscious of doing so myself. A few weeks later, a debonair medical resident introduced himself to me. Like a big bunny, I intentionally wrinkled my nose several times. This time it certainly didn't provoke the same kind of comments. He probably thought I had a mild seizure disorder. My Grace Kelly/Ingrid Bergman moment had clearly come to an end.

At times I feel my femininity is somewhat suppressed. While recently flying home from New York, I felt like a *bona fide* Alabama redneck. I was in so much pain from my backpack that I took three aspirin without water. Across the aisle from me was a slender and manicured blond. She had a leather briefcase that did not bulge and a slim billfold-size leather purse on her shoulder. How poised and confident she looked in her silk above-the-knee suit with perfectly matched hose and Italian leather shoes. By contrast, I was sitting with a bag of dried hydrangeas, a golf umbrella, and a purse that had the dimensions of a carry-on. My backpack was full of French-white Corningware that I had bought at the Corning factory and books from a library sale. My back was throbbing, my lips were quivering, and people kept giving me pitying looks as if I was a poor novice traveler. I knew I'd be fine with a bottle of painkillers and a good night's sleep, but in my current state I could only envision additional humiliation, such as having my underwear strewn out across Pittsburgh as we flew over. (I had stuffed my underwear in boxes of books I ducktaped together.) I opened my journal and wrote: *"The only positive thing so far this morning is that I haven't run into my husband; or if I have, I'm sure he didn't recognize me as **the one**."* I closed the journal and prayed that the Lord would get me home with what dignity I had left. Perhaps in this case my femininity would have been enhanced by staying away from the library sale and out of the hydrangea bushes.

What Is It Anyway?

If femininity were about wearing lace, smelling rosy, and acting delicate, I would be sunk; however, dressing appropriately and being neat in our appearance is important. It's really more how we act in what we wear than what we actually wear, but clothes must be important or there wouldn't be so many verses in the Bible about them. Though I can feel just as feminine in my hiking boots and jeans as I can in a Laura Ashley dress, getting too comfortable and careless in my appearance is a temptation that I have had to learn to guard against. The majority of my working life I have worn surgical scrubs and, though scrubs are already comfortable, I used to wear mine huge and baggy. Once while I was coaching a sixteen-year-old in labor, my scrubs fell to the floor. I was so intent on our breathing exercises that I didn't even realize what had happened until my legs got cold. There was nothing mysterious about me that day, especially since our labor room faced the entire nursing station.

I exposed my mystique by accident on this occasion, but I've noticed that some women are more deliberate. Recently I attended a lingerie shower for a friend from college. It was the usual fur-throwing, feather-flying sort of event that is always a lot of fun. The next day I saw this girl at a Christian event and thought she was wearing one of her new pieces! Without exaggeration, it really could have passed as lingerie. Yes, all major parts were covered but not much more. We live in a society that encourages us to believe that being generous with what we reveal of our skin is feminine, when, in fact, the opposite is true. For a woman to dress in a revealing or seductive manner only detracts from her femininity.

I am not suggesting that you dress like Mother Teresa (unless, of course, you live in India). Your clothing reflects your style whether it is classic and traditional or trendy. We all love talking about Mrs. Proverbs 31 and it certainly sounds like she did not dress dowdy. Pick and choose the things that make you feel attractive, not seductive, and focus on styles and colors that enhance your best features. (You will *never* catch me in a pair of hip huggers.)

Weight watching is an inescapable issue in our society that is plagued by both obesity and anorexia. Mark my words, the Renaissance look will *never* return. Though we all have busy schedules, eating well and exercising should be one of our priorities just like your mother said. And a good multi-vitamin is always a good idea. Who can deny that we are at our optimum when resting properly and in good shape physically? But in the event of a "too-tight" crisis, the new and updated spandex undergarments may at times be our best friend!

Similarly, a warmly decorated home enhances our femininity. Be it a dorm room, a shared apartment, or your own house, your home reflects your spirit. It should not be decorated according to anyone else's taste. Be yourself: eclectic collections, Victorian lace, brass and glass, or Elvis and leopard; your style is your own. I live in a small cottage that is my little corner of the earth to fill with things that are special to me. By filling it with pretty colors and fresh flowers, I have tried to create an atmosphere that is warm and inviting. We should cultivate this God-given, feminine desire for a home that is a place of peace and rest.

Miss Fix-It

Unfortunately, for many of us the process of getting our homes to a place of peace and rest can be anything but peaceful and restful. In fact, it can be a source of discouragement in our quest to achieve that elusive feminine "mystique." Without a husband to help me around the house, I have had to assume the role of a handyman, and it's hard to feel like a lady when you're firing up a lawn mower, revving a chainsaw, or using a bathroom plunger. Even the purchase of these items is hard for me. I don't like to spend my money on such things. I'd rather buy a pretty, scented candle or something for the kitchen.

My toolbox is a testimony to this ongoing struggle. Every single girl needs one, of course. Mine looks different from the typical male toolbox, though. For starters, it is a discarded file box, filled with my "tools" of choice: duct tape, super glue, and an assortment of nails. Almost anything in my house can be fixed with duct tape and super glue. When I must resort to nails, I drive them in with a wooden-sole clog instead of a hammer. It's called the creative art of carpentry.

As unskilled as I am with tools, you would think I would like new homes where you just move in. You don't have to pull up carpet, sand floors, or replace windows. Oh no, not me. I like old houses, the ones with character and charm. The houses that deplete your checking account and make you cry from exhaustion and frustration. On a tearful, "I wish I lived in a new condominium without character" kind of day a few years ago, I decided an electric drill would dramatically improve the quality of my life. But when I walked into Lowe's hardware, I discovered an entire department devoted to electric drills, with hundreds to choose from in every shape, size, color, and price range. Overwhelmed by the selection and already exhausted and covered with paint and sawdust, I felt tears spring to my eyes.

At that moment, a nice, innocent-looking teenage employee walked up smiling. "Hi, ma'am!" he said with enthusiasm. "Do you need some help?" Biting my trembling bottom lip, I managed to say in a slow and quivering voice, "I (sob) just (sob) need (sob) to buy a drill (several sobs)." His smile suddenly disappeared, and he started backing away *slowly*. With a very nervous voice, he said, "Just a minute, ma'am. Let me get you some help." *Oh, great,* I thought. *I am having a nervous break down in Lowe's.*

Maybe I was indeed crazy. Only the day before, in an effort to remove the seventy-five-year-old tile over the pine floors in my kitchen, I had decided to rent one of those monstrous machines that looks like what road construction workers use to break up asphalt. This massive, reverberating, powerful turbo machine had me literally backed into my kitchen cabinets when a neighbor heard my cries for help and rescued me by pressing the "off" button.

I just didn't grow up doing all those things around the house that men traditionally do. Little things that are nothing for some people can become monumental tasks for me. For instance, I once struggled at least an hour trying to change a fluorescent bulb that seemed too long for the light fixture in my kitchen (no dumb-blonde light bulb jokes, please; I'm a brunette). Finally, I shrieked in frustration, and the bulb fit. Similarly, I was never thoroughly convinced of the necessity of changing the filter in my air conditioner, until Dad eventually convinced me of the importance. Actually, I just said, "yes sir" but I'm still not sure why they need to be changed. There are only about 1100 sizes to choose from, and finding the right size was the first major hurdle.

But every six weeks now I drag out my little kitchen stool and change my filters.

And ultimately, when I enjoy the coziness of my cottage by myself or with friends, I know that the frustrations of this single woman masquerading as a handyman are worth it. Not even the manliest of jobs can destroy the essence of my inner femininity. Recently, for example, I had to pick up a big rental truck to move some furniture. Trying to combine this errand with a special event for which I had on heels and hose, I found myself driving down the highway in a huge, non air-conditioned truck, grinding gears in Italian pumps. I smiled and said to myself, *"Now here is a REAL woman!"*

Pure and Feminine

Real womanhood is a concept that has suffered terrible distortion in our very permissive society. The so-called liberation of women, as an outgrowth of the sexual revolution, has made promiscuity both acceptable and expected of our gender. Single Christian women frequently take some heat for sexual purity. Just as many find it difficult to believe that we can't be feminine without décolletage, we also have to *deal* with those who think we are lacking in our femininity if we are not participating in compromising activities. Your average visit to your gynecologist may go something like mine typically does: the coldness of the hard examining table permeates the large paper towel you have vainly attempted to wrap around you. It's the *once-a-year ritual* of being squeezed and poked by a man who is not your husband. While you are in your most unladylike and undignified position, he starts the typical barrage of questions.

"Are you pleased with your birth control? Any side effects?" he asks.

"I don't use birth control. And no, no side effects," I answer.

"Well, surely your partner uses protection," he questions.

"I wouldn't know," I reply.

"Are you not concerned about getting pregnant, Angela?" he asks concerned.

"Don't you still have to have sex for that to happen?" I retort.

75

You finally reach a point when you feel like saying, "If I have to repeat myself one more time, I am going to put that speculum in your ear canal and open it up, so you can hear me loud and clear." You have been there—you and your little paper towel.

I recently called my endocrinologist about a concern I had. After the usual assessment questions, he asked if I thought I might be pregnant.

"No sir, I am not," I answered.

"Angela, are you sure?" he asked.

We had been through this scenario before, and he knew that my marital status had not changed. I was silent.

"No sir, I am not pregnant. I am sure," I answered again.

"Your hesitancy is not very convincing," he said.

What he didn't know was that I was struggling to keep from saying, "Sir, remember way back in Anatomy and Physiology when you studied reproduction? Well, unless The Basics have changed, I know I am not pregnant." Instead, I quietly and simply said, "I am not pregnant."

"Well, nevertheless," he replied, "a pregnancy test would be a good idea." Hanging up the phone, I laughed, "I give up!"

Sometimes you don't have to advertise your chastity to become a topic of conversation. I happen to have a lot of non-Christian friends for whom this is always an area of intrigue. Ironically, they worry about pregnancy or STDs, though they claim to be perfectly comfortable with their promiscuous lifestyles. Now that really makes a lot of sense. And as I mentioned earlier, if you work in a secular environment, you may find yourself the object of genuine curiosity too. These taunts and gibes may make you feel left out, but don't forget that true womanhood and femininity are founded in a pure heart. Smile with them as if you know something they don't. You do.

Of course, many single women have regrets about their pasts. They have shared their hearts and bodies in what turned out to be broken and painful relationships. If you desire to know purity in your heart and your life and have asked the Lord to forgive you, be assured that He has. Look not into the past but rather into the face of your Redeemer. Allow His grace to cover your sins and restore pureness in your heart.

Several years ago, I lived with several wonderful Christian girls. One of the girls had lived a very promiscuous lifestyle. But when she became a Christian, she embraced *all* of Jesus, including His cleansing and renewal. Her life exemplified purity and gratefulness for His redemptive work in her life. She blushed more easily than we did and was the model of feminine mystique.

Interacting with Men

As we embrace a lifestyle of femininity in our appearance, behavior, and attitudes, we will find we become more confident in this role God has patterned for us. We may also find that men are confused about their masculinity and may not initially treat us as we wish. I truly believe that if women will simply act like women, men will eventually begin to treat them as such. Perhaps after a generation of women's lib, men are not quite sure just what women want. Elisabeth Elliot tells a story of her brother, a college professor, who stepped back to allow a female student to go in front of him while holding the door for her. She turned around and angrily said, "Did you open the door for me because I am a lady?" "No, because I am a gentleman," he responded.

Another gentlemen friend recently married a woman who was infuriated when he opened her door for her early in their relationship. As president of a successful law firm, she enjoyed her independence and didn't think she needed help getting into a car. He didn't disagree with her, but he never stopped opening doors for her. He continued to treat her like a lady, and she finally started acting like one. The strong emotional walls around her crumbled as he lived out his masculinity and won her heart. Fortunately, he had insight into what was behind her fortress of protection, but not every man would persist in the face of such rejection.

Whether men are courteous to us or not, we must not allow their weaknesses to become ours. Be sure to give an encouraging "thank you" if a man holds the door for you. And if he doesn't, don't be so eager to point it out. Our aim is to be consistently gracious in every circumstance, even when others are not. This can only happen as our expectations of others are yielded to Him and our responses are tempered by the Holy Spirit.

The Taming of the Shrew

Indeed, we must make the consistent choice to grow in our femininity. I once heard Elizabeth Elliot ask for a show of hands of women who were born with a quiet and meek spirit. There were no hands—only laughter. We can be so very sweet, filled with love, kindness, and meekness while the fruits of the spirit fall from our branches as we feel their delightful squish beneath our feet. But we also have the opposite capacity. I laughed the first time I saw Elizabeth Taylor and Richard Burton in Shakespeare's *The Taming of the Shrew*. I so beautifully identified with Taylor's magnificently played role that I actually thought I could have rivaled her performance. At the end of the play, the shrew surrenders and is gentle and sweet in her response to her husband. Perhaps if I had a Richard Burton, I'd shape up too, I thought.

Shakespeare is not our only source for information about shrews. The Bible also contains numerous examples of "contentious" women, along with the exhortation not to allow ourselves to be among them— no matter what our hormones are doing. We can't go around blowing people away with our words and blaming it on our moods. The reality is that no one forces us to react with rage; we choose to react in this way. And just as we can choose to be sharp with our words, we can choose to be kind. And if we can't be kind, we can be silent. My journal bears witness that even I can be victorious in this regard: *"I kept my mouth shut tonight,"* I recently wrote at the end of a stressful day. *"Thank you, Father."* People and circumstances provide many opportunities for us to react from our temperament or to respond in a spirit of grace.

What is in our hearts is often revealed with what comes from our mouths. We must make daily and conscious choices for godliness in our speech. This most definitely includes our tendency to gossip. Gossip reflects poorly on our femininity and on us, whether we find ourselves in the company of men or women. As a woman with two sisters and having worked the last thirteen years in a profession that is dominated by women, I know something about the slandering fairer sex. I've noticed that we sometimes find it difficult to respect the differences in others and to focus on that which is good in them. Sadly, I could write a whole book on how I have failed miserably with my mouth and attitudes. Miserably.

Many years ago I asked the Lord to let me always be honoring to others and trustworthy with my mouth. I noticed I began to walk a greater measure of obedience until I figured out a way to cheat. There have been times when I wanted to get the "scoop" or some hot detail about someone but didn't want to appear to gossip. I found that asking an "innocent question" in a group of women was all I needed to do to get the group talking. I didn't have to make a single contribution; all I had to do was sit there with my saintly self and soak it in. But somewhere along the way I realized that *that* is as deceitful and wicked as slandering someone.

Years ago, I sarcastically commented that maybe I should just cut out my tongue and end my misery. But I am sure I would have become just as fluent in sign language. I think there must be a root that goes from the backs of our tongues to the Garden of Eden. More recently, it has become a practice of mine, before walking out the door each day to pray as the psalmist did, "Let the words of my mouth, and the meditation of my heart, be acceptable in thy sight, O Lord, my strength, and my redeemer." Ask the Lord to give you tenderness toward others **before** you even open your mouth.

That's not always (or ever) easy. An acceptable trend in modern conversations is to speak about issues that used to be private; there is far too much openness and freedom of conversation about intimate and modest issues. Advertisements for everything from contraceptives and underwear to the hottest new feminine products are customary and people discuss in gory detail an adulterous affair as if they were talking about the weather. We speak with familiarity about issues that should be regarded with respect as private, especially in the area of intimacy. Draw boundaries in your conversations, especially with men. Rabbi Manis Friedman, author of *Doesn't Anyone Blush Anymore?* once made an insightful comment to me worth noting, "Modest conversation protects intimacy and is the framework that nurtures it. Keeping intimate issues covered preserves the beauty of the nature of intimacy."

A guarded tongue, heart, and behavior will definitely enhance our femininity, which has more to do with inward beauty than with outward appearance. My prayer is that each of us will walk in a fresh surrender in our attitude toward femininity. Only by His grace can we be transformed into the image He intended by the renewal of our hearts and minds.

While we are learning to find our true identity as women of God, let's remember that identity—that feminine "mystique"—does not come from our outward appearance (although we have seen how that might enhance it). It comes from our attitudes, our relationships with others, and—most importantly—our relationship with Christ. As we desire to develop our womanly and inner beauty, we would be wise to look not to *Ms.* magazine but only to our Designer.

Chapter Five

MORE THAN VAIN IMAGINATIONS

"The real voyage of discovery consists not in seeking new landscapes but in having new eyes."

— Marcel Proust

If you have ever had the experience of using a Turkish toilet, you know that they have a direct sewage line to the depths of Sheol. While you are using these facilities, you think for a moment that you might be there. Frequently called a "squatty," it is a hole in the ground with surroundings of which I will spare you the details.

Laughing is a good option because it is the last place on earth that you would ever want to be nauseated. On one of these cultural adventures, while traveling in a very primitive part of a second world country, I pondered what I could do to lighten up a rather overwhelming scenario. One of the kindest guys I have ever known, Jay, had sweetly accompanied us girls and was standing outside patiently waiting for us. Already known for his weak stomach, he was beginning to be overpowered by the combination of scents from dead fish, live poultry, and this ancient Turkish toilet. While inside the facilities I wondered what I could do to help divert Jay's five senses from the sickening smells. Muffling my laughter, I sent one of the girls out to tell Jay that I had dropped my clog into the deep, dark, descending hole and would he please come and fetch it for me? I am sorry I didn't have the satisfaction of seeing his distressed and contorted face. His reaction of horror and a desire to be helpful produced peals of laughter for us the rest of the trip.

Imagination is one of God's most wonderful gifts to us. Not only can it help us survive the intoxicating fumes of a Turkish toilet, but it can also transform otherwise dull or even tragic circumstances. Roberto Bennini's award-winning movie, *Life Is Beautiful*, tells the story of a father who used his imagination in a concentration camp to shield his son's mind from the horrors of the Holocaust. He skillfully created a captivating adventure while weaving a beautiful life story in the midst of tragic elements. Bennini attributes his gift of imagination to his father, whom he said used to create fantasies and escapades to deflect his children's minds from their impoverished circumstances.

Many people, such as Joni Erickson Tada, rely on the sustaining power of His grace and the gift of creativity to go about their daily activities. Joni provides a real-life example of someone who has used God's gift of imagination to overcome tremendous obstacles. A quadriplegic since the age of eighteen, she has allowed great physical challenges to become a springboard into ministry through her paintings, writings, songs, and encouraging words. Most of us do not face the physical hurdles that many people with physical disabilities, such as Joni, deal with daily. To my friends who must deal creatively to accomplish what may be a mundane task to some: may you continue to be refurbished with clever and resourceful ideas. And may you know day-to-day encouragement. I also pray that none of us will ever be in a concentration camp or even have to visit "squatties" on a regular basis. However, we know a creative imagination can help us turn challenging circumstances into favorite memories, come up with creative ways of blessing others, and elevate our level of worship to our Creator as we see the world through His eyes.

I once sent a card to a friend that said, "For your birthday let's celebrate by doing something wild and different: Let's get together and NOT talk about men!" All single women can relate to "hen parties," where discussions about their male counterparts abound. While these conversations can be hilarious, they are a sad reflection on how we spend our time and what motivates us. If all our creative focus is centered on men and getting married, how interesting are we?

Fulfilling Life

Too often women postpone dreams and great ideas while looking and waiting for *him*. I have put a couple of my own ideas on hold in the past, so I understand better than I wish I did. But we are feminine creatures of creativity, born to use this God-given gift. Awakening our senses to the world around us and developing our imagination can provide some of the most fulfilling experiences that life has to offer. We will enhance our relationship with the Creator as we see His fingerprints surrounding us.

Focusing on imagination at first may not appear to be "spiritual," but God obviously thought variety and beauty important. If He had not, we would live in a gray world, and flowers would not have colors or fragrances. Instead, a most wonderful and creative God formed us. In Him we *live* and *move* and have our *being*. Part of our *being* is not simply in physical living, but in our minds and in our imaginations. In a generation in which imagination is often squelched, it's good to assess your life and evaluate where your interests are. Does your life consist of many things other than eating out, shopping, television, and movies? If not, you risk being a dull and stagnant woman, rather than a fulfilled one.

Strolling through a quaint side-street in Edinburgh last year, I read a sign in a shop window read "Hold onto life with both hands." I could not help but think that many are barely holding onto life with two fingers. Their hearts are beating and there is breath, but in conversation you sense they are bored and immune to wonder. There is no "fullness of life" in them. In his book *Traveling Light*, E. Peterson writes, "For all our elaborate expensive fantasies, the actual lives that most people live are filled with impotence, boredom, and obscurity." Does that description fit anyone you know? Hopefully not you, for there is an infinite source of imagination and creativity within you. Dormant perhaps, but nevertheless it is there waiting to be discovered.

Each of our personalities is wonderfully diverse, and what gets my imagination stimulated might make yours shut down. Pray that you would have eyes to see and ears to hear what your creative Father would say to you about your imagination. Pray also that He would show you anything that has created dullness of heart, preventing you from hearing His heartbeat and enjoying His world and its beauty. No one could have said it as well as Helen Keller: "It is better to be blind and see with your heart, than to have two good eyes and see nothing." And as the Father opens your mind and awakens your soul, write down some of the fresh thoughts that come to you.

Cultivating the mind and the imagination is like potty-training a child; pretty soon it will become natural, but until that time, we may have to be reminded occasionally. I have discovered several ways to stir the slumbering cells of my soul. The first has to do with getting quiet. Many years ago, Miss Helen Wright said to me, "Angela, quietness will never come knocking on your door but everything else will." Then she showed me numerous Scriptures pertaining to quietness. Isaiah 26:20 particularly spoke to my heart: "Enter into thy chambers and shut the door about thee; Hide thyself for a little moment."

Since that day with Miss Helen, I have embraced the truth of this verse, though at times I have had to get creative in doing so. Several years ago, for example, I went through a period when my house somehow had a special cloud of invitation over it. I could not escape people dropping by day and night. I even tried hiding my car and that did not work. Taking the message of the above verse literally one day, I went into my closet with Bible and journal in hand and wrote: *"I have discovered the most wonderful place. It's in my closet and I am finally alone. No phone calls and no distractions. It's a little cold so I will have to dress warmly."* How is that for desperation? I grew to love my daily visits to that little closet. I could hear friends and neighbors knocking at my door or walking in if it wasn't locked. I sat there smiling quietly.

You don't have to literally get into your closet to fulfill the mandate to "hide yourself." My life just seems to naturally take the extremes at times. (But if you have never spent time in your walk-in closet, you might try it!) Your spiritual retreat may involve several days away, a simple overnighter, a hike in the woods alone, or just an evening of turning off the phone. My telephone used to be a terrible enemy of quietness in my life, and the idea of not answering it would send me into emotional spasms. It was actually easier for me to go away for a few days than to stay away from the phone. Once while I was waiting for a salesperson in a department store, the phone at the counter rang. After several unanswered rings, I picked it up. I just could not stand to hear a phone ringing desolately. You are thinking, *now that is ridiculous.* I could not agree more.

Like the phone, television can also prevent us from hiding ourselves. When I got rid of my television a couple of years ago to devote more time to studying and writing, some of my friends were horrified at the loss of my animated companion. But I loved the contrast of peace and quietness that replaced it. What about you? Are you comfortable with silence? Can you read or eat a meal without the accompaniment of the television or music? Sometimes you even need to turn off your Christian music and just think, pray, or read in silence.

As we hide ourselves quietly, we become aware of the things that nurture our creativity and imagination. Each of us is different and therefore nurtured by different things. In my times of quietness, for example, I have discovered that for me a fireplace is about as important to a home as a bathroom. Perhaps my enjoyment of a good roaring fire or the glowing embers is a bit extreme, but that is just one of the things that helps to feed my imagination. Somehow the atmosphere inspires thoughts and ideas in me. Arrange times for daily quietness in your own life, and find out what inspires you. The Lord will shower on us times of refreshing, if we will be still long enough to absorb them. On occasion, of course, your quietness may get squeezed out by unavoidable chaos. Never fear: His grace abounds. In the midst of hectic activity, you can draw on the imagination you have been cultivating in your hiding place. So on those days when life is a zoo regardless of your desire to be quiet, just become one of the animals and enjoy it!

"Never despise mundane events: they can be doorways to profound spiritual understanding"

— Lucy Shaw

People-Watching

Another way to nurture our creativity is by observing people. Why does the work of Norman Rockwell appeal to the tender and poignant parts of our hearts? The reason is simple: Mr. Rockwell had a way of noticing the ordinary events of our lives and capturing them in his wonderful paintings. His portrayals of common experiences and everyday people help us to appreciate what we sometimes overlook. We too can develop that ability to see the wonder of the ordinary by taking the time to look beyond a person's skin and hear beyond his words. Become sensitive to other people's emotions and you will experience emotions and sensitivity within yourself that you may not be aware of.

I have always found the study and observance of people in everyday settings to be not only a quiet and reflective event, but insightful. After attending a friend's dinner party, who was not a Christian, I spent a great deal of time thinking and praying, and later recording my observations in a journal entry. *"Tonight at a party I enjoyed listening to the conversation around me. Actually I did not so much enjoy it as I was intrigued as well as saddened. Such pretty people. Such empty words. I believe people are so hungry for someone who will listen that when they sense you are genuine in your interest, they will open up to you like a book. You quietly listen as they turn the pages of their hearts to you."*

The many hours I have spent in airports have provided some of my favorite journal entries. I remember a conversation with a woman who was flying to her daughter's funeral. I listened and shed tears with her and prayed. On another occasion, I was privileged to watch a family receive an adopted Chinese baby girl. Four excited children and parents gathered around this little one, and their radiant smiles and tears were a gift to my day. I couldn't help following them at a distance, sharing in their joy and wiping tears myself.

Listen with more than your ears and see with more than your eyes at the airport, the grocery store, on the street, and even at work. *"I so enjoyed my post-arteriogram patient today,"* reads another journal entry. *"He was a retired newspaper editor who had lived and traveled extensively in England during the war. He told me fascinating stories of his life and travels. Neither of us could go anywhere since I was applying pressure to his surgical site for two hours so he wouldn't bleed to death. We made the best of it and had a wonderful time together. I was quite sad to tell him good-bye when he was transferred to another floor."*

Become an observer of life around you and a listener to those events that are actually deeper than words. Hear the emotions of the heart, and see into the eyes of the soul. Wherever we find ourselves are people who need to be listened to, reached out to, and cared about. As we observe people, we develop not only our imagination, but also sensitivity to our surroundings and the capacity to look beyond ourselves to meet the needs of others.

I have observed (for whatever it is worth) that people who are easily bored must lead rather dreary and monotonous lives. Certainly there is no excuse for such a dreadful malady! To begin with, there is an infinite number of unexplored thoughts for your thinking pleasure— this in and of itself is an event for which you could be pleasantly occupied for hours upon hours. In addition to enjoying the art of enjoying great thoughts there are almost as many great books, and vast venues of music, art, and other cultural mediums to provoke your imagination.

Music of the Heart

"Music is enough for a lifetime, but a lifetime is not enough for music"
— Sergei Rachmaninov

My musical repertoire while growing up was Christian in all varieties. Each was wonderful in its own way. I've always been especially moved by the ancient hymns of my faith that proclaim honor and praise to Him on whom my foundation is built. Over the years I have collected a rather impressive amount of praise and worship songs that is almost ridiculous in its enormity. And sometimes in the past, it seemed that I frantically filled every waking minute of my life with Christian music.

In recent years, I have also begun to understand the deposit of beauty that God placed in the souls and minds of the great composers.

I always enjoyed classical music when I was exposed to it, but I often didn't take the opportunity to pursue listening to it as I do now. My neighbors, Harold and Mary Brown, an elderly couple who played with symphonies professionally in their younger years, have assisted me in this pursuit. When I first moved into my current home four years ago, I would hear exquisite melodies drifting from their open windows while I was outside working in my yard. The music of Mendelssohn, Brahms, and Rachmaninov was as nurturing to me as I was to my plants and seedlings.

Great music not only touches our souls, but it also inspires us to worship our Creator. Edith Schaeffer describes this sort of inspiration in her book, *Restoring Crescendos to Your Prayer Life*: "One of the best times of adoration to the Lord was for me listening to a live perfor-mance of Debussy's *La Mer*. I was practically screaming inside my head: Now I know what the stars sounded like when they sang together before creation!" Albert Einstein said of Yehudi Menuhin, a child prodigy who was playing in concert halls at the age of seven, "Now I know there is a God!" And my own sister shared that, at her first sym-phony, tears unexpectedly sprang to her eyes at its beauty.

Many classical composers wrote music specifically for Christian hol-idays and worship services, some of it under the direct inspiration of the Holy Spirit. George Friedrich Handel composed the well-known oratorio *Messiah* in a mind-boggling twenty-four days. After complet-ing its magnificent "Hallelujah Chorus," he is said to have been moved to tears, telling his servant, "I did think I did see all Heaven before me and the great God Himself."

Ingrid Trobish tells of when she and her husband Walter were living in a thatched hut close to a dusty African village: "We made sure we had good books in different languages and some kind of music. We had a little wind up phonograph with three records we'd rotate and a small pump organ and when we were able to get family instruments Walter started a family orchestra." They were nurturing and protecting the beauty of their souls from the heat and dryness of their surroundings.

It has been said that classical music helps the heart move. That was certainly the case for me one night. Sitting alone at a chamber music concert, I was completely smitten (for two hours anyway) with a short little cellist because of the passion and expression with which he played. I was reminded of him when I read Niccolo Panganini's quote: "I am not handsome but when women hear me play, they come crawling to my feet." I didn't crawl, but I did enjoy!

I am not saying that classical music is the only thing that can awaken your imagination and senses. Country, rhythm and blues, big band, or something else might set your heart singing and your feet dancing. Bluegrass music and banjos always make me want to clog. Though I don't know how to, my nieces and I sure have fun trying! Whether it's Mozart, James Taylor, Willie Nelson, or Twila Paris, expand your musical horizons and maybe even explore learning a new instrument or pursuing a vocal talent. Let music do for you what Berthold Auerbach once remarked, "Music washes away from the soul the dust of your everyday life."

Beauty in the Books

"The love of learning, the sequestered nooks and all the sweet serenity of books…."

— Henry Wadsworth Longfellow

The American card designer Mary Engelbreit has captured the spirit of Longfellow's quote in a picture of a young girl in a cozy little nook with book in hand. I have always loved snug places with an engrossing book. In fact, as a child I spent many pleasurable hours reading by flashlight under the covers. I would do the same now if I didn't have autonomy over the light switch in my bedroom. My books are like treasured friends. Once one of my roommates was attempting to help me create extra space in my little bedroom. "Why don't you put some of your books under the bed?" she asked innocently. Genuinely hurt, I replied, "That would be like putting *you* under the bed."

Sometimes this love for books has gotten me into trouble. I can spend hours in old book stores and can't resist those annual public library sales—even if they're out of town. Last year, while in New York on a nursing assignment, I bought four boxes of old classics for a few dollars, without considering how I would meet the luggage weight restrictions on my flight home. When I arrived at the airport with my treasures, the man behind the ticket counter greeted me with a scowl. He clearly had no appreciation for fine literature. After grumbling, fussing, and fuming, he agreed to a mere fifty-dollar surcharge. Of course, that was before he saw my massive oversized carry-on. I smiled—or was it a grimace—as I limped past him toward the plane. Once on board, I began downing painkillers without the benefit of water, and for a moment, questioned the wisdom of my book purchases. However, when I look at these friends on my bookshelves, I know they were worth the pain.

My first and greatest adventures abroad were in reading. The friends I have made as I turned the pages of their lives, and the wonderful literary journeys I have taken, helped me develop a love for travel and a desire to see people and places that are new. In short, they have provided one of the most important stimuli for my imagination and provoked the desire for travel.

There are many wonderful Christian authors in this generation. Read their writings, but I would encourage you not to limit yourself to their books. Get to know the old classics too. I believe strongly that good literature can provoke thoughts toward God. Sometimes those who are on the outside looking in may have more insight into where we are as Christians than we have ourselves. The difference between a great book and a mediocre one is simple: trashy books inspire trashy thoughts, and good literature provokes great thoughts.

Bill Bennett, author of *The Book of Virtues,* suggested several years ago that people today are impenetrable to moral philosophy but will respond to moral literature. His book went on to become a bestseller, a fact that tends to support his premise. *Invitation to the Classics* is another recent publication with essays by Christian scholars on classic literature. These authors encourage us as Christians to engage in culture by reading good literature. If you are not currently reading a book that is a real classic, other than the one that you are holding in your hand (I'm kidding), I would encourage you to begin one. *WORLD* magazine recently gave a partial listing of the best titles proclaiming or applying a biblical worldview in a hostile twentieth century. The fact that not all of the books were by Christians did not exempt them from the list. I have since then reread *The Diary of Anne Frank*, and the insight and depth of this thirteen-year-old made me feel like a romance writer. I was deeply provoked at this young Jewish girl's perception of life.

"How wonderful it is that nobody need wait a single moment before starting to improve the world."— Anne Frank

A good children's book can be a wonderful jump-start to your imagination. I have almost as many children's books in my home as I do "grown-up books." C.S. Lewis unwittingly helps vindicate me in my love for children's literature. He points out that "no book is really worth reading at the age of ten which is not equally worth reading at the age of fifty. A children's story which is enjoyed only by children is a bad children's story. The good ones last"

So instead of sitting in front of your television, try spending an evening at the library or at a great bookstore with a coffee shop. From travel books to biographies, there will surely be some wonderful titles that will captivate you. For a change, try browsing in the children's section of a bookstore or library. The *only* misfortune is that the seating section within the children's books is too small to be comfortable! I'm always hauling an armload to a more comfortable adult section. Reading circles are becoming increasingly popular which is a nice option if you are slowly weaning yourself from your animated companion. You don't have to toss your remote control, but you might find that picking up an old classic might be a new and refreshing page in your life.

Language of Love

"For my own part I never had the least thought of turning Poet till I got heartily in Love and then rhyme and song were in a manner the spontaneous language of my heart."

— Robert Burns (1783)

I laughed when I read that it wasn't until the Scottish rose, Robert Burns himself, was smitten that he became eloquent in what is considered the language of love. Fortunately, we do not have to be in love to enjoy poetry or to write it. I have often been disappointed in myself that I didn't love poetry as I felt I should, and that I seemed to get lost so easily in it. Even the great poets have never provoked the appreciation I felt they should have.

However, I have noticed recently that many poems that I have read at random strike a pleasant chord somewhere in my heart and lift my thoughts higher. Perhaps I am a little more in tune with life. There is a poet of this generation who expresses my heart, life, dreams, and desire for God in a way that I cannot articulate. Her name is Ruth Bell Graham. After reading her collection of poems, *Sitting by My Laughing Fire,* for the first time, I decided to establish a habit that I have practiced repeatedly since: curling up in front of a nice fire with her book of verse in one hand and a cup of coffee in the other.

I do not consider myself a poet, but on occasion I feel a leap of spontaneous words and pull out the closest piece of paper. When I read my poems later, I either laugh, roll my eyes, or savor the moment that inspired it all over again. One such moment occurred several months ago when I was in Scotland. Lying in the softest grass I'd ever seen, atop Arthur's Seat, the highest point in Edinburgh, I felt an urge to indulge my poetic inclinations. I noticed two birds perched on a mound a few feet away, and what really caught my attention was the way they kept turning their heads toward each other and appeared to be having a conversation. There was a sweetness, almost an intimacy, about their dialogue. Unfortunately, I had just used my last picture, photographing myself in the grass while holding the camera at arm's length and pointing the lens toward me—it turned out terrible. But thankfully, the poetic picture I captured of my feathered friends was clear as the Scottish skies.

February 13th: The Eve of Valentines Day

Today I'll be a Scottish lass, while lying in Arthur's arms of grass
Softer than an infant's kiss; I close my eyes in peaceful bliss.
I awaken and see in front of me two birds with hearts of harmony;
Close together beak to beak, they move their heads in synchrony.

They know 'tis the eve of Lovers' Day and together back and forth they play.
Far in the distance sets the sun but not on these sweethearts that beat as one.

My feathered friends have made me smile under these bonnie blue skies.
I bid them goodbye as together they fly
to the dusk of the hills where their nesting home lies.

For darkness comes in many ways but where there is Love, the darkness cannot stay.
And though I lie here all alone and dark is closing in, my soul is filled with Love and Light, until that eternal Day.

As you grow in your ability to observe the world around you, learn to express your observations creatively. Poetry provides a wonderful outlet for our imaginations and a fresh way to acknowledge God in His creation. Try putting your thoughts on paper. They don't have to have rhyme or meter, and I believe you will not only enjoy but be surprised at what flows from within.

Monet and Millet

"A work of art introduces us to feelings we have never cherished before."
— Abraham Heshel

Like classical music and literature, great works of art can inspire us to worship God. While visiting a friend recently, I was drawn to a picture in her living room. After I'd stood silently in front of it for a few minutes, she began to tell me about its history. It was a print of the French work *The Angelos* painted by Jean Francois Millet. *The Angelos* represents the call to worship three times a day. It depicts farmers in the field whose heads are bowed reverently in the midst of their work, as they stop to give thanks. I was deeply provoked by the humility portrayed in their faces and posture.

Some artists can plumb the depths of the Scripture; in fact, their interpretations may give us new insights as expressed by songwriter Allen Levi, "He reaches our heart through our eyes." Henri Nouwen tells of his experience when his heart and soul were touched by art in his book, *The Return of the Prodigal.* Nouwen describes a revelation he had as he contemplated Rembrandt's *The Prodigal Son* at the Hermitage in St. Petersburg, Russia. He sat for hours in front of the painting in the changing light, reflecting on the parable as Rembrandt had cast it. He recounts that not only was he stunned by it's majestic size, but gripped with an intensity of his soul far beyond his anticipation as he contemplated the embrace of father and son. Through his encounter with this magnificent painting, Nouwen's heart was enamored by the tender and overwhelming love of his Father as well as identifying with the weakness of the son.

Like Nouwen, I have at times stood in silence in art galleries, drawn to the Creator by the expression of an artist. Every great artist expresses the gift that God has placed within him, whether or not he acknowledges the Giver. A few years ago I admired a work of art by a friend who does acknowledge God as the source of her talent. To my delight she later gave me the admired painting, which now hangs in my bedroom.

It appears to be a scene in Scotland and has exquisite clouds, the kind you want to get lost in. I had not yet been to Scotland when I received her gift, but the clouds that hang in my bedroom reminded me of God's beauty and the verse, "And the clouds are the dust of His feet." As Ruth Bell Graham said, "Even the dust of His feet is beautiful." I daily receive a great deal of pleasure from this lovely painting. Not only is it beautiful, it is a reflection of His beauty.

Don't Miss the Dance

"Dancing is the poetry of the foot."

—Dryaan

Ingrid Trobish remembers her husband Walter explaining to her the importance of dance. He felt that pious, religious people needed to get in touch and find harmony with their bodies. Since that wasn't part of Ingrid's missionary training, she wasn't particularly comfortable with the idea, but she must have thought it worth investigating. "While Walter was away on a six-week trip," she wrote, "I spotted an advertisement for a dancing course in Salzburg. I got a babysitter for the children, drove off in my little Volkswagen, and learned the Vienna Waltz alongside Austrian farmers. Dancing set free something in my soul—and in my children's, like skipping and hopping after being tied up for a long time."

My own experiences with dance are similar. My mother enrolled me in ballet as a child with the hope that it would help me to become more graceful. While it didn't seem to have had that particular effect on me, it did awaken something inside of me. In recent years I have taken several adult ballet classes, not intending to perform on stage but simply because I enjoy it. After this book hits the press, I expect to be bombarded with invitations to perform, but the answer is "no."

If you have never danced alone in expressive movement, then perhaps you would be pleasantly surprised. You certainly don't have to be trained, but maybe you would enjoy an adult studies course. I dance alone all over my house. (Not having living room curtains at the moment, I've been dancing in my bedroom of late so as not to provoke the curiosity of my neighbors.) And, of course, you don't have to be married or romantically attached to dance with someone. (I would hasten to add that when I talk about dance, I am referring to the type of movement you would be comfortable doing if your parents or someone like Billy Graham were in the room.) I learned how to ballroom dance on a basketball court with my friend Mensor. Dancing with Mensor is an experience, because he is legally blind. When he twirls or dips you, you never know where he might swing you or what he might grab in the process.

Winning first place at the Knoxville Mardi Gras Ball may not have been my greatest achievement, but it was certainly one of the most fun. My date and I went as Rhett and Scarlett—only I was the Carol Burnett version, swathed in yards of green fabric, with a curtain rod sticking out across my shoulders. When I complained that my date was not swinging me enough, he informed me that every time he did the curtain rod kept hitting him in the eye. He thought he was such a Casanova because he spoke a little French and could make Cherries Jubilee; but if he had really wanted to get my attention, he would have risked his life for me.

Dancing before the Lord as a part of worship has many biblical precedents, but Christians in the West tend to be more self-conscious about this form of worship than those outside our culture. I was reminded of this during a trip to Guyana several years ago. While the rhythmic beating of the bongo drums filled the room in which we were worshiping, my Guyanese friends swayed to the music in their brightly colored sarongs. And there I was in my blue and white dress feeling a little dull and stiff. Our voices swelled in harmony, as we celebrated the end of our training. I had grown to love these beautiful people.

Suddenly my friend Obena stepped out in the aisle, and with her lovely brown eyes closed, oblivious to all around, she began to worship in dance. I was aching to dance, as others joined in with her, but I was afraid of what the team would think. In a few minutes, though, my desire to enter into worship overcame my inhibitions and I began to sway with them. Somehow my movements weren't as fluid as theirs, and sensing my frustration, one of the sisters caught me to her and with her lovely British accent gently said, "Flow with the spirit, honey; just flow with the spirit." I don't think I have ever "flowed" quite like that since then!

I remember watching a woman who was paraplegic worshipfully express herself with her hands. Though we were watching her, our attention was pointed to the One she was worshiping. Your body can be used as a means of expression in a pure and wholesome way. Katrine Stewart once said, "Keep your soul dusted and your heart dancing through music." Now surely *that* is the greatest dance of all...the dance of the heart.

Life through the Eyes of Children

In addition to silence, people-watching, and the arts, time with children does wonders for our imagination. Why is it that the creativity of a young mind frequently surpasses that of an adult? Unfortunately, we have become too sophisticated in our thinking; therefore, we often miss the wonder of the world around us. It is a wise adult who can learn to think as a child and see life through her wonder-filled eyes. Time spent in conversation with and in the company of a child whose imagination has not yet been dulled by thinkless activities is a creative event in and of itself.

I've heard that the average four-year-old laughs four hundred times a day. Knowing the incessant giggles of my own nieces, I have no trouble believing that. Children aren't concerned with our social statistics and they aren't weighted down with responsibility, nor should they be. But if we shared even a little in their ability to laugh spontaneously, we would be happier and healthier. Surely the Lord thinks laughter is important, because He created our bodies to respond to it by releasing chemicals called endorphins, which promote good health.

C.S. Lewis says the Lord wants us to have a child's heart, but a grown-up's head. We can have the maturity that an adult should have as well as childlike joy. Children never postpone the feeling of joy or wait for a more appropriate moment to express happiness. They live in the present. Even after a good spanking, they seem to bounce right back into action.

If you have the good fortune to spend time with children, you will notice that they have a way of adding the oil of life to our rusty minds. Recently I left some of my rust behind in the ditch of a Carolina mountain. My niece Caroline and I spent the afternoon careening down a mountain in North Carolina at breakneck speed in her little red wagon. When the speed got out of control, we plowed into the autumn leaves in a ditch below and lay there giggling. Take every opportunity to "rust-proof" your life with children.

Children are loyal and quick to forgive. They smile and laugh easily and are spontaneous in their affection and trust. They delight in things that we often overlook, like rolypoly bugs, lizards, and ice-cream cones. You can hear the quick little intake of breath and see their eyes widen with amazement as they examine new and colorful crayons or watch leaves float down the creek. Their laughter is contagious. Make opportunities to spend time with them; you will see the world a little more clearly through their eyes. Be assured that sometimes they see much more clearly than we do.

Cake and Candles

"Life begins when you get one."

— Angela Payne

Children love to celebrate their birthdays. A lot of adults, however, have lost that enthusiasm. They have forgotten that life begins when you get one—a birthday, that is. That's why I love to use my birthday as an occasion for childlike creativity. Remember, I am a "maxed-out" sanguine— the party waiting to happen, as John Trent says. As a rule, I never work on my birthday and I make sure to vary my celebrations. For my thirtieth birthday, for instance, I decided not to have a big party like a typical sanguine would have. Instead, I spent quiet time in

Kentucky at a Shaker village. It was just what I wanted: a day of quietness with journal in hand on a farm with lots of sheep.

Another year when I was in Israel and my birthday approached, I thought the most wonderful thing I could do was to go to Tel Aviv and watch the Russian Jews arriving at the airport. Since it was during the Gulf War, I loaded up my gas mask and caught a bus to Tel Aviv. Unfortunately, I couldn't find any Russian Jews, but I still had fun eating kabobs and humus dip while wishing myself *"Mazol Tov!"*

I have to say, though, that my last birthday was the best, as far as uniqueness. I was in Uzbekistan with friends, and we went to the ancient city of Samerkand for the weekend. We had a wonderful day shopping and spent the evening in a Turkish sauna with intermittent dips in a cold pool. I then had the luxury of a massage by a Russian masseur. It was a new experience for me and I have a suspicion that it was for him as well. By the time he had slapped and kneaded and walloped me with all of his Russian gusto, I have to admit I was pretty relaxed. A shot of his Russian vodka and I would have been history. I wobbled back to the rest of the team, where a wonderful surprise party awaited me.

You don't have to go to another country to have a great day. The important thing is to use your imagination and celebrate! Don't allow being single to dampen your enthusiasm for this very special day. I have even given a couple of parties for myself without telling any of the guests beforehand that it was my birthday. When they all arrived I yelled "Surprise!" At the one for single girls only, I pulled out a pack of Old Maid cards.

I also like to look at birthdays the way that others look at New Year's Day: a time for reflection and goal-setting. About ten years ago I heard and began following an interesting suggestion: on your birthday, write yourself a letter of the things you would like to happen in your life in the coming year; on your next birthday, read it. For the first three years, when I reread the letter, I simply wrote "Ditto." It was disheartening. By the end of year four, however, I am delighted to say that many of my desires and goals had been fulfilled.

Other Special Celebrations—Besides Every Day of Living!

In addition to birthdays, the calendar is full of opportunities for creative celebrations. Holidays furnish wonderful occasions both to enjoy and to reach out to others. Fortunately, I grew up in a family who extended invitations to those that had lost a spouse, singles without families in town, new immigrants, and international students. Everyone without someone was welcome, including the husbandless like myself.

Go through your calendar and think of imaginative ways to bless other people. On Saint Patrick's Day, one of my friends throws a big party with all the oysters and beer you want. Although it's wild and as spiritually dark as you can imagine, I go so that at least one source of Light will be there. In fact, I try to attend parties that I am invited to for that very reason. And I think it's important as a hostess to use theme parties or holiday gatherings as a non-threatening occasion to invite both Christian friends and friends outside "the holy circle."

I've found that one way to make someone else's birthday or anniversary special is to organize and write "skits" that offer a playful look at his or her life. I have quite a collection of wigs, hairpieces, costumes, and props that I have accumulated over the years from such productions. Birthdays, graduations, rehearsal dinners, the joy of losing weight—in short, all special occasions—offer a unique opportunity for some friendly satire. In fact, when I die, I will not be surprised if skits are performed at my funeral.

The last major dramatic event in which my friends and I participated was in honor of my friend Mary Virginia Reese's engagement to Ron Sommer. I dubbed it "The Sound of Mary" and feel sure that Rogers and Hammerstein would have been proud of my adaptation of their somewhat better known musical. Apparently, Ron's mother has circulated the video recording of this one all over Atlanta, bringing hope, cheer, and hysteria to multiplied viewers.

It turned out to be providential when one of my friends gave me her wedding dress years ago. I now have to use duct tape to hold it together, but it has been essential in all of our past wedding productions, traveling with me far and wide. Once one of my friends was visiting me from

Oregon. While putting his suitcase in the trunk of my car, he saw the box labeled "Wedding Dress." "Boy, Angela," he remarked, "you are *always* prepared." From the reenactment of courtships with all the creative details, to the celebration of the life or accomplishments of someone, skits are a wonderful way to bring encouragement, affirmation, and laughter.

Even if you end up spending a holiday alone, use your imagination to make it special. One year I had to work not only on Christmas Eve but also on Christmas Day. Though I was disappointed about not being with my family, I still wanted to celebrate and worship at a Christmas Eve service, as I love to do. I was unaware that I would face some obstacles along the way. I took a change of clothes to work and left the hospital in time to make a midnight service at an Episcopal church. I got on a one-way street— going the wrong way— in downtown Birmingham. At five minutes till midnight, a police officer trying to make his annual quota wrote me up for a traffic violation. I was not in a mistletoe sort of mood when I wished him a Merry Christmas.

Finally seated in the sanctuary, I found my surroundings cold and dry. I seemed to be meditating more on my traffic citation than on the gift of Christ to the world. There was also the distraction of the elderly man sitting in front of me wearing green polyester pants with big red poinsettias scattered all over them. Instead of leaving the church with a reverent and worshipful heart, I left feeling like a dried-up Christmas tree. I arrived home well after midnight to a cold and dark house. My roommate was gone; I was alone. Though our gas logs put out noxious fumes and smoke, I lit them, feeling desperate for warmth in my soul. Curled on the couch in something warm and fuzzy, I sipped hot chocolate and sang Christmas carols alone. Sipping and singing, I began to feel that warm and wonderful joy of this special season. Reading the Christmas story aloud I then went to bed before getting a headache from the gas fumes. I had an early morning Christmas breakfast with Miss Helen before going to the hospital. That holiday stands out as one of my most meaningful and memorable holidays, and it had nothing to do with the mistletoe headband that I wore to work.

Everyone celebrates in different ways, and I think it's important to establish traditions in our celebrations, even if we are single. One of my traditions is finding a "Charlie Brown Christmas tree" rather than a large and perfect one. I have loved the imperfections of my trees; in fact, the last one stayed up until February. I refused to take it down until I completed my Christmas cards.

Valentine's Day provides another opportunity for creative festivity. This particular day on the calendar sometimes serves as an unpleasant reminder to single girls. But instead of feeling left out, why not use your imagination to celebrate this holiday, too? I was in London one Valentine's Day, and all I can remember about that day is that there were red boxer shorts and white ones with red hearts in every store display. I thought they were delightful and wished that I had someone to buy them for. The next year I bought a red nightgown and wrote a poem.

This Valentine's Day I celebrate with joyful bliss
Because surely a box of Godiva is better than a kiss.
Though wise King Solomon said kissing was fun
He'd been sipping from stomped grapes that had seen too much sun.

From my two pounds of chocolate, I will take many bites
The panel with the listing of fat grams I will keep out of sight
Hoping that soon after the last delectable swallow
The man of my dreams will be quick to follow.

These days of good clean living without men and kissin'
Just keep me from knowing what I am missin'.
The princess of Christian romance: Grace Livingston Hill is fine
Read everyone of her books, all 109.

Now book learning is good I do agree
But there is another part of my education that I can't see.
It won't come from books or a thesis from a university,
I think the time has come that I earn my MRS degree.

Instead of allowing Valentine's Day to remind you of your marital status, make it into something fun. Have the girls over or send out children's Valentine's cards to your adult friends. This special day is always a fun opportunity to celebrate with loved ones and those who need to be loved.

Whatever you do, don't postpone joy! Though some celebrations are planned, such as baby showers, weddings, and birthdays, others can occur spontaneously. When I left my job as a nurse to begin writing full-time, I was taking a big step in following one of my dreams. Wishing to mark the occasion with a celebration, I bought the wildest set of sheets filled with all the flowers, swirls, and colors that you have ever seen! These are the sort of sheets Monet would enjoy sleeping in after painting his *Water Lilies*. They still remind me of the day I made a step forward in my life.

Howl at the Moon

"The sky is the daily bread of the eyes."
—Ralph Waldo Emerson

I have not yet landed in cow manure, but my days of lying in cow pastures are far from over. Lying in grass and looking up at clouds gives me an innate sense of pleasure. There is a pasture across from my parents' home in which I spent many hours as a child. An occasional nap or a look up into the sky was always nice. That love for big brown-eyed cows and grass has carried over into my adult years. When I reach the age of maturity where such childish behavior is inappropriate, I will stop. But I seriously doubt that it will ever happen.

A few years ago, I discovered firsthand that the British must not take naps in the grass. Walking along the banks of the river Thames at Cambridge, I decided to sprawl out in the grass to read and watch the swirling clouds until I got sleepy. I later woke up to a proper "Billy" standing over me and speaking into his walkie-talkie. I can still hear him saying, in his strong English accent, "Oh I do say sir, there is a young girl lying in the grass. No, really she is. Yes, she appears to be breathing. Shall I awaken her?" I could see his befuddled face from behind my sunglasses and was about to burst out laughing. Finally I sat up, resisting the urge to invite him to join me.

Now what do lying in grass and sleeping have to do with imagination? Well, it's just one of the things that I do that seems to keep me alive. It has nothing to do with narcolepsy. I'm the same way about stars, but especially **big fat full moons**. After studying a particularly beautiful moon one night, I wrote in my journal: "*I stood silent and in wonder at one of the most unusual moons tonight. It was perfectly round and full and had what looked like an illuminating rainbow around it. Exquisite. And I heard You say, 'Be still and know that I am God'.*"

One night, after a meeting with some international students, an American guy and I were strolling across a college campus. We came across a Malaysian friend who had fallen asleep on a large stone wall. He woke up and talked with us for a while. We left and my American friend asked, "What in the world was that crazy guy sleeping outside for?" "He was looking at the stars and fell asleep," I said. "Don't you ever go outside late at night and look up at the stars?" "Not when I can be sleeping," was his reply. I had already surmised that our lives were headed down different paths, but that insightful comment was all the confirmation I needed. My path is one with many stops along the way to see the stars and sleep under the moon—and even howl at it if I want to.

There are *so* many times that the sight of a full moon has been a revelation of God's sovereignty. These have provoked words of worship and at least one wonderful occasion of laughter. Several years go in Israel, a knock on the kitchen door startled me as I was peeling vegetables. I was in deep thought about the Gulf War. Tension was thick between the Americans and Palestinians because of American aid to Israel. The ministry I was involved in was on the Mount of Olives, so we were surrounded by Palestinian neighbors, and I had spent many evenings with my neighbors across the path drinking tea. When I answered the door, I found Ali, one of my tea-drinking neighbors. With his deep Arabic voice he beckoned me outside. Solemnly and with reverence, he pointed to the full moon. "Look into the face of the moon, Angela, and tell me what you see." I had never seen one like it before nor have I since, but I truly did see the faint outline and shadow of a man's face in the moon. Wow!

"Ali," I said excitedly, "it *really* is the man in the moon! Wow!"

"Yes," he agreed somberly. "It is the face of a man. Whose face is it, Angela?"

Studying it intently, I said, "It is... it ...is ...why I'll be! It's the face of George Bush! It's George!"

"No!" he declared. "It is the face of Saddam Hussein."

"It's George!"

"No! It's Saddam!"

By that time we were both laughing, though Ali hadn't meant to.

I started spending more time looking at stars after I got my basset hound puppy, since I often walked him at night. Having Oscar has made me slow down a bit; I spend more time sitting in the grass and looking at the stars. I smell the fresh air more lingeringly. And isn't it sweet to watch the responses that adults have to an innocent puppy?

The key to enjoying life's simple pleasures is to enjoy them **now**. My good friend Delma has mentored me in this skill. She has groomed me in the art of naps and picnics. She carries her portable picnic basket in her car for emergency picnics. Who else would overnight me fresh spring flowers from her yard with the stems secured in zip lock bags and ice cubes? Not only did her enthusiasm over spring hyacinths and daffodils make me laugh, but I enjoyed them for several days!

I once visited Delma in the little community of Stewart, Mississippi, which is like going to see the Waltons. I was admiring the barn that she and her husband and son had just built, and I especially loved the loft she had fixed up under the slanted tin roof, complete with an old iron bed and cotton linens. I knew what she had in mind. Hours later when I shrieked, *"It's raining"* and went tearing down to the barn, she of all people understood that I had not lost my mind but was going to indulge in the luxury of an afternoon nap in the rain under a tin roof.

I completely and utterly love the sound of rain. And in a good storm, I am useless for anything except reading, writing, or sometimes just listening.

When my niece Caroline and I are together and it's raining, she now comes and sits on the porch with me and watches and listens. At a torrential downpour just recently, my sister pulled Lydia's diaper off and she played in the rain to her heart's content. I have a feeling she is always going to love the magic of rain. One of these days, I just might pull my diaper off and join her.

Cultivate an appreciation for simple pleasures. They are God's countless gifts to us and come in every variety. Your ability to notice and enjoy them will benefit your own heart, as well as enhance the imaginations of those around you. My friend Jim made me aware of the wondrous power of such ability several years ago. The two of us were walking along a cobbled street in the Ukraine, where we were doing short-term work with university students, when I mentioned to him how much I enjoyed walking in my clogs on cobbled streets. The happy clackings of my leather and wooden clogs on those ancient stones made me feel deeply joyful. Jim looked thoughtfully at me and said, "You know, Angela, I like that about you. The darndest things make you happy."

That was the greatest compliment to me. Jim was old enough to be my father; he was seasoned and wise from years of law practice. We had had rich conversations about his experiences as an attorney, his extensive travels, and his farm in Missouri. Jim has that subtle fragrance of life like the good smell of leather from an old book. I have never smoked a good cigar, or even a bad one for that matter, but my conversations with Jim gave me the kind of satisfaction I imagine a good cigar with cognac would give. He had a perception of life that I wanted to be able to share, and my respect for him remains deep. Yet here he was admiring my ability to be happy with the darndest things. I took it ultimately as a compliment for my Father, who has given me the capacity to appreciate the little, subtle joys of life.

Waking Up to Your Dreams

I have had some absurd dreams, and that was the extent of them: absurdity. But there are some dreams that we should pay attention to. If they are recurring and lingering, perhaps they are dreams that need to be pursued. I'm not talking about a dream that you have at night but a dream of the heart. Whether it is to travel, pursue another profession, or learn another language, follow that dream.

While shopping one day at a nearby mall, I stopped on the second floor to look below and listen as an inner-city youth choir sang. Tears sprang to my eyes as they enthusiastically sang "Follow Your Dream." "Yes, Father," I prayed, "let each of their young hearts follow their dreams. May they not be stopped by poverty, discouragement, or lack of nurturing their desires." And you, my friend, may you not let fear or doubt stop you from following those longings from within. May He give you the courage and wisdom to pursue the dreams He is awakening in you.

When a delightful coffee shop opened near my home, I commented that the only thing I didn't like about it was that I didn't own it. For almost ten years, I have dreamed of owning a coffee shop where people can have all the coffee and conversation they long for. I want great books and comfortable chairs for my patrons' reading pleasure. It will be filled with fresh flowers and warmth. Perhaps it will soon be the time for me to take steps to bring this dream into reality. What a dream come true—drinking coffee all day with the girls!

Several of my dreams have come true while others are still sleeping. One of mine is to go to Paris and have my hair cut. After seeing the movie *Sabrina*, I knew I had to go to there. You see what a good hair cut did for her! My brother-in-law confirmed this desire in a note he sent me: "Paris has been known as the city of love for hundreds of years. Maybe it can do something with you. One can only hope."

What are the dreams of your life? Oliver Wendell Holmes said that some people die without their song being sung. Don't let your songs remain unsung. Sing the dreams of your heart and don't delay the joy they will grant you. The fulfillment of some dreams may take longer than you want, but be reminded of Psalm 138: "The Lord will accomplish what concerns me." But often we have to cooperate with Him as we follow His prompting.

Remember in speech or English classes when you had to do a collage of your life? It was one of my more enjoyable assignments at the time. Now I constantly have one in progress in my study—which spills over onto my refrigerator. It is a combination of pictures and clippings from magazines. Actually, our entire lives are an ongoing collage. The things we do, love, and feel are an expression of who we are. A couple of years ago, a friend spent many hours going through magazines and cutting out pictures that expressed her life as it was then and the things she desired to happen. Even now, some of the biggest dreams represented in her collage are taking place in her life. It is a simple thing to do but very revealing. Know what your dreams are, so that you can begin to pursue them creatively, and be open when the door of opportunity knocks.

Developing our imagination and using the gifts that God has given us can help to direct our thoughts away from the sometimes all-consuming topic of marriage. More importantly, though, they can lead to times of spiritual renewal and refreshment, as we learn to see the world and the people in it the way our heavenly Father does.

I heard John Guest say that he prayed "Lord, take my mind and think through it." If we could see the world around us as God does, I believe it would seem like fresh water to our stagnant minds. Often we overlook the most profound things in our desire to see the spectacular. How interested in life are you, and how interesting are you as a person? Is there anything that stirs your soul or awakens your imagination other than the thought of marriage? If not, I encourage you to dip into the refreshing pool of imagination and renew your mind, regenerating some of those brain cells that you might not have used in a while.

Once when I arrived home after having been away, I found a bouquet of pink tulips waiting for me with a note from my dear friend, Tara. "Welcome home, my precious friend! I have missed you and prayed for you daily: for new eyes and a renewed heart and for new adventures in our friendship, as I glimpse a bit of the wonder of what God is doing in you. I love you!" The message of that note is what I pray for you, my friend: new eyes for the world and the people around you, a renewed heart in Christ, and lots of great adventures in a new walk of wonder.

Chapter Six

CHAOS

Caroline wrapped her arms around my neck and looked around uncertainly. We observed the flurry of motion as children raced from one bright machine to another. The light fixtures were the only things that didn't seem to be moving. The sounds of bells and buzzers, beeps and clangs, whirring and shrieks filled our ears. Uncertain of what to do, I joined the line of adults. I had not a clue as to how many tokens I should buy for one little girl to play a few games and eat pizza. Tapping the shoulder of the man in front of me, I shouted, "Is there an orientation to this place? This is a first time for us."

"Oh really?" he yelled back. "I come here once a year for my daughter's birthday." He motioned to a blur of movement streaking past with pigtails and pointed to the number of tokens he thought I should purchase. He was next in line and I saw him walk away. "Thanks," I called out, though I don't think he heard me.

I watched the transformation of my three-year-old niece. Initially, I had to encourage her to begin using her tokens. In about fifteen minutes, she was as out of control as every other over-stimulated child there and was similarly running around in a frenetic state with a glassy look on her face. The sweet, shy, uncertain disposition of my niece was only in the recesses of my memory. Struggling to get her attention, I cupped her face in my hands in a feeble attempt to get her to calm down. She could hear me with her ears but there was no getting in there. The external stimulus had overloaded her.

I saw myself clearly in Caroline that night: frenetic, out of control, over-stimulated. I was trying to do every good thing and not accomplishing much more than being exhausted. Sadly, my journals have often reflected this lifestyle of chaos. Even now I sometimes feel as if I am a lightning rod for life's chaotic events. The day Mount Saint Helen erupted, I just happened to be flying overhead with some friends in a small engine plane. I refused to take the blame for that event, though it was suggested by those with me.

Princess of Mahem

All my life, I have tried to cram too much into my schedule, leaving too little time for the commitments that I should have been focused on. This continues to be a struggle for me at times, so as I write from my past and present experiences, keep in mind that I am still learning. My journals over the years reflect the consequences in my life as I have said "yes" to a multitude of wonderful and even Christian activities. In actuality I was really saying "no" to time alone with God or to taking care of necessary personal affairs. Many of my experiences have had severe repercussions, and often I feel I have been a tattered reflection as a Christian. At times I have felt my life has not displayed the characteristics of a daughter of the Prince of Peace, but rather the ruling and reigning *Princess of Mayhem*.

A person who has taken the dictum *Carpe Diem* with a little more gusto than was meant in its challenge to "Seize the Day," I have nearly had seizures in my quest to enjoy life. My friend and fellow nursing coworker, DeeDee, who has known me from the beginning of my nursing career, made an acute observation of me several years ago: "Angela, if you don't slow down you are going to crash and burn." She had seen me on more than one occasion flying into work breathless from running across the parking lot and bounding up the stairs. On this particular night, she did not realize how discerning her comment was.

Unbeknownst to DeeDee, my commute to work that very evening had substantiated her concern for my life. Catching a late flight into Birmingham, Alabama, there was just enough time to drive an hour to the hospital where I was scheduled to work. I had not allotted myself time to change clothes, so passing all cars in sight on the interstate, I set my cruise control and reached to the passenger seat for my nursing uniform.

112

Pulling my shirt off, I quickly slipped my dress over my head while holding on to the steering wheel with my knee. After shimmying my pants off one leg at a time, I reached for my support hose (now, maneuvering nursing support hose in the dark while driving is a little more challenging than regular hose—I've done both). Making good progress and staying completely on the road, I might add, I pulled into my hospital parking lot in time to reapply my lipstick, brush through my hair, and slip on my nursing shoes. DeeDee was innocent in knowing how significant her "crash and burn" comment was and she had no idea what I was going to be doing when I left work the next morning. Driving to my parents' after a busy night at the hospital, I transferred my suitcase to my sister's car and Sunnie, Shawn, and I set out for a wedding in New York. One week later, I returned home in time to change, take a shower, and speed out the driveway to the hospital where I worked a double shift. At the time it just seemed to be the normal thing to do in order to reach my travel goals. No different from anything else I ever did.

My mother who watched similar scenarios over and over, quietly prayed. She prayed that I would see what this lifestyle was doing to me physically and emotionally, but also spiritually. When she would try to talk to me about the need to slow down, I would defend all the good things I was doing. She would strategically place articles in my reading view on the consequences of stress and the need for quietness and rest. Though I appreciated her concern for me, I knew she didn't understand the "importance" of my activities. What she did understand so very well was that my quiet time was in snatches and spurts and it was reflective of the chaotic life I was leading. I'm not denying that I didn't enjoy much of what I was doing, but my journals indicate much of what I was feeling: *"Lord, do you remember the three stranded rope from Ecclesiastes? I feel like two strands of my rope are frazzled and frayed. That is me. The other one is You and it is strong. I am going to wrap around you before I completely unravel."*

In my attempt to accomplish an unrealistic amount of activities I became accustomed to living a "running and churning" lifestyle, as described in a newsletter for The Christian Medical Ministry by Earle Carpenter. "The running and churning person that jumps over Proverbs 8:34: 'Blessed is the man who listens to Me, watching daily at my gates.' "A tumultuous lifestyle will eventually take its toll emotionally and physically, as evidenced by the number of current studies on the physiological effects of stress on bodies. As Christians, this physical stress will eventually spill over into our spiritual lives.

I have made some of my impulsive decisions when I have been so busy "running and churning" that I couldn't think or hear clearly. It's difficult to be hysterical and Spirit-led at the same time when emotions are full of clamor and there are voices from every direction. The process of making even simple decisions when your mind is in a state of turmoil can turn into a fiasco. On one of those mornings I was hyperventilating about a travel decision that needed to be made in a few hours. Unable to think or talk clearly I called my friends Scott and Victor and asked them to pray. Having warned them that I was on the verge of female hysteria, both were quiet as I spilled out my frustration and confusion. A moment of silence followed and then Scott said, "Thanks Ang for calling. You have just helped me to make the decision to be celibate." Fortunately they were unscathed by my emotional outburst and are now happily married.

Running on Empty

For years, I heard the quotes such as "The good is the enemy of the best" or "Be aware of the tyranny of the urgent." Though hearing, I never listened. Occasionally warning signs went by unnoticed. Once in preparing for an international trip, I boarded the plane completely exhausted. In attempting to tie up the events of two weeks, I had slept and eaten very little in the previous three days and was looking forward to sleeping for several hours in flight after the meal was served. When the gourmet chicken in wine sauce hit the bottom of my empty tense stomach, my speech became slurred, and I couldn't sit upright from the dizziness. I literally had to be assisted in stretching out on the floor where I slept for eight hours without moving.

I would like to say that I learned my lesson from that experience but I'm afraid that I didn't. A journal entry shortly after that event reflects what was in my heart: *"It is sunny and bright outside my window and spring is bursting in life and color and freshness. Yet, there is a pounding rain inside of me against the windows of my soul. A dark storm brewing in which I fear a tornado forming. I am sensing the impending havoc and devastation already. My life is torn asunder...things pulling and pushing and shoving rudely. Back and forth I am pulled. Please breathe on me your breath of Life and bring the peace and stillness that follows the storm."*

Two years later when preparing to have surgery, my physician had encouraged me to rest emotionally and physically to enhance an optimum outcome. I was awake the entire night before trying to catch up on things before my hospitalization. By 5:00 in the morning, I was actually looking forward to general anesthesia so I could sleep for a few hours. My surgical procedure involved removing my thyroid gland which was malignant. There were several months of follow-up treatments in which I went through what I called my "Embalming Syndrome." For the first time in my life I could do little more than rest, as I was completely physically depleted. After several months when my endocrine system began to get in order, I jumped right back into the cyclone of life. Everything the Lord had been sharing with me about quietness was forgotten in my quest to catch up on all I had missed.

Why the Chaos?

Each of our reasons for leading a frenzied life will in all probability vary according to our backgrounds and personalities. My most outstanding weakness, though granted *at times* can be a strength, is that I enjoy doing so many things. Life is sometimes like a day at Baskin-Robbins to me. There is such a variety of wonderful events to choose from and more numerous than the classic thirty-one choices. As in eating too much ice cream, unlimited activities will put you into overload. In a recent conversation, a friend was sharing that her husband helped to build boundaries of protection around her from over-commitment.

My heart felt that twinge of longing when she said that. I have often wished for a husband to protect me from myself. As singles without the responsibility of a family, we may take our free schedule as a license to use our time as we desire, rather than asking for divine guidance. Though I don't have a physical husband, I do have the Holy Spirit to guide me and assist me in saying that *huge* two-letter word when needed. *No.*

Another weakness that is a little more difficult for me to address is simply called "The Ego of Angela." Many times I have said "yes" to commitments merely because of recognition and accolades that I knew would be generously showered upon me. (I hope you realize this is killing me to say this. However, *that* part of me needs to die!) In my accomplishment of many rather formidable tasks, I have "humbly" shunned the praises showered upon me while savoring every sweet morsel of the compliment. That sort of motivation is full of pride and hypocrisy. As I once heard songwriter and speaker Allen Levi say, "The only thing that matters at the end of any accomplishment is that we hear the applause of the nail-scarred hands." If our motive is less than this pure desire and rooted in our ego, we have been misguided in our purpose.

Sometimes loneliness can cause a person to fill the void with people, activities, and the accumulation of things. I am reminded of the words that Pascal once said, "There is a God-shaped vacuum in every heart." If there is a barren place deep within you that is longing to be filled, I would softly encourage you that only as you know God personally and intimately will that need will be met.

Certainly I believe we are to seize life and all the opportunities He desires for us. But the "commas and periods" of life are as important as the exclamation points. *"Life has been so scrambled, so full of good things, places and people. Why do I allow this to happen Father? How many times will I allow all of these good things to separate me from you? I have been spending time with people and activities and none with You. Please help me be free of all that entangles me."*

If our lives are filled with so many events that intermesh, eventually we will feel the entanglement of them. Most likely we will trip and fall, and usually in the process the consequences affect others as well. People will naturally begin to expect these sorts of behavior patterns. In relation to this thought, several years ago I began to have the growing desire that my life would reflect the truth from Proverbs, "A good name is to be chosen above riches." A good name speaks of one that returns library books on time and takes the time to pay bills on schedule. These may appear to be small issues, but in reality they pertain to character. A good name speaks of one that is not habitually late and is trustworthy and doesn't make rash commitments. A good name reflects a life that is tempered and not out of control. So often I feel that when my name is mentioned, everyone braces themselves for some sort of chaos they expect will follow. As many times as I know I have frustrated others, I feel sure that no one has been more so than me.

As is the case with many disorganized people, getting anywhere on time has always been a challenge to me. Several years ago, I attended the funeral of a friend who had died unexpectedly. The pastor lightened the mood briefly when he said, "This is the first time that Brenda has ever been punctual for an event she was expected to attend." *That's what they are going to say about me,* I wryly thought.

Procrastination is another one of my struggles. A rather impressive quote that I wrote in my journal several years ago states: *"Procrastination is the art of keeping up with yesterday."* How can we do what He wants us to do today if we are still in yesterday? Sometimes I procrastinate out of fear that I can't accomplish all that is required, and sometimes I just procrastinate out of habit. I would rather not have to address this sin that I have petted and held close to my heart. Procrastination is delayed obedience to things the Lord speaks to us in His Word or even in the prompting and leading of the Holy Spirit. It doesn't matter that we don't want to obey. Obedience doesn't require our understanding or approval. Assuredly, delayed obedience always brings consequences. *"Father, of all the things in my life that I long for, I pray most that I may cultivate instant obedience to the issues you have spoken to me about. I have developed habits of procrastination that are selling my life short of the standard You have for me."*

117

Procrastination can keep us from pursuing goals in this life, but it can have eternal consequences as well. One of the most crushing experiences I have ever known is when I went to pick up a former roommate and noticed that our neighbor's condominium looked empty. Mary and I had spent a lot of time in conversation with our neighbor and were waiting for the right moment to ask her about her relationship with the Lord. I "meant" to go back and see her after I moved out. She died only days before, without waiting on me to come back and see her.

As I have heard my Father say to me, "Behold, I make all things new," I can freely offer you that hope as well. I have fallen on my face so many times, it is a wonder I have a nose left. The only nice thing about failure is that you land at the foot of the cross. After falling, I have not landed in a graceful heap, but rather a big splat...in a hundred broken pieces. Be assured that when that happens you can lie there in all of your brokenness or look up. If you look up, you will see God's hands, see His face, hear His voice, and feel His heartbeat. He loves me in all of my brokenness, and as I reach up to Him, He brings me to His heart. I am a daughter of my Father. You are my sister, a daughter of our Father, and He loves you with tenderness, passion, and grace.

Different Lightning Rods, Same Chaos

In my circle of single friends, I have found that most of us face chaos of one sort or another. Perhaps in your case, the lack of balance is in eating, spending money, or even in the realm of over-commitment to a job or schedule. I have friends who *never* struggle with being on time; however, their rigid order and structure prevent them from having the freedom of an open heart and home. Should an unexpected guest drop by, for example, these people are uncomfortable setting an extra place at a table whose dinnerware and meal might be less than perfect. They often despise their own personally-imposed constraints and wish they were more flexible. Maybe you are like them and emanate the essence of organization: punctual, predictable, never coloring outside the lines. Both of these are extreme areas of chaos to Him. Through seeking the Holy Spirit, He is then free to take our scattered and fragmented lives or our ordered, predictable, and scheduled agendas and bring *divine order* into our chaos.

Remember that God, in His sovereignty, has made each of us different in temperament, personality, emotional makeup, spiritual gifts, and capacities. For instance, I alluded to my "lightening rod" sort of personality. Perhaps you are the type of person that can stand in a lightning storm and experience nothing but a chill. On the other hand, others of us seem to attract those unexpected bolts out of the sky even when the sun is shining. I have tried to no avail to assess how these things happen and my only profoundly deep and theological answer is that "I don't have a clue."

My conflict with an ordered schedule is compounded by the most bizarre events that confirm that I am indeed a "lightning rod." I know on more than one occasion my nursing co-workers must have wondered if I was making these stories up. One morning I awoke to find that my dining room roof had caved in. I called in to the hospital to say I was going to be a few minutes late. On another occasion, I called from the hospital elevator emergency phone to say I was there but couldn't get out. Still another day I jumped into my Trooper, reached to close the door, and for some unexplained reason, no amount of tugging, pushing, kicking, or yelling would budge it. I drove to work with the door wide open, trying to avoid sideswiping things in my way. Fortunately, it was early in the morning before the rush hour traffic. In a conversation with friends recently, they said that my readers would undoubtedly think I was exaggerating about my life's events. Let me reassure you. The only thing I exaggerate about is my weight.

The encouraging theme in my life even in relation to all of these lightning-rod experiences is that He has a wonderful way of causing good to come out of them. For example, because of all the chaos I have lived with all these years, when a little extra event takes place, I typically stay unusually calm. Whether during an unexpected medical emergency or the inevitable unplanned chaos that happens while traveling in foreign countries, I have found slow deep breathing works better than hyperventilating. I tried to explain this philosophy to a former

119

roommate who was not accustomed to calm reactions in tumultuous situations. One day while casually putting out the small fire from a burning dishtowel on the stove, I asked her how her day had gone. All she could do was shriek and run around in panicked circles.

Chaos and Consequences

I remember perhaps my greatest night of darkness when the Lord had to drag me out from "under the bed" to get my attention. The sweet reminder of God's unconditional love for me followed a time of chastening. Its story of His grace and mercy in my life will always remind me of this undeserved love. Almost three years ago, as I buckled Caroline into her car seat, she looked up at me with eyes of anticipation.

"Are we going to McDonalds, Sissy?" she asked.

"No honey, Sissy has to go to court. And I hope that since you are with me I won't get thrown into jail." I answered. She was only three so she just laughed, knowing that she and Sissy always had such fun together and assuming that this was another adventure. I didn't explain the predicament I was in. I just made sure we both looked cute.

A few weeks before, I had been stopped for speeding. The nice officer had come back to my car after taking my license for a few minutes and asked: "Ma'am, do you know your license has been suspended?" My hysterical outburst of tears clearly indicated to him that I did not. In my disordered lifestyle, I had failed to get around to changing my new car title into my name. Consequently, I had not gotten a tag renewal notice and had not bothered to walk to the back of my car and check the expiration date, like apparently some people do. In my opinion, people that have time to walk to the back of their cars and look at their tags need a life or at least a hobby.

The suspension apparently happened after I had tossed the notice for a *previous* speeding ticket into a to-do pile and had not taken care of it. Sometimes I cry demurely and ladylike, this was not one of those occasions. Faced with the serious consequences of my procrastination, I was devastated. Quite frankly, I believe the only reason I was not sitting on my posterior end in a police station that night is simply because of the kindness and compassion of this officer. He was not supposed to let me drive with a suspended license. My drive home was darker than the night that surrounded me, and I could hardly see for my tears. During a very long evening until early the next morning, I continued to sob while berating myself for my failure to take care of even simple things. The next day I was too ashamed to tell anyone except one close friend who offered to drive me to work. Fortunately, after a great deal of expense and proper legalities, my license was renewed.

Yet I still had my court hearing to face, and I couldn't help but be grateful to have the moral support of even my three-year-old niece who was visiting me from out of town. As Caroline and I drove into the parking lot, I was surprised to see an old friend who was an attorney. He was so glad to see us and was calling the meeting providential even before he knew my situation. He had not been in that particular courtroom in several months and "just happened" to be there that day. Quickly surmising my predicament, he volunteered to represent me free of charge. Within an hour, Caroline and I left the court to celebrate God's undeserved mercy toward a guilty but loved Sissy.

Even such a serious and humbling event could not protect me from one of those "lightning rod" experiences. Before the hearing, I stopped at a vending machine to get Caroline a treat, bent over, and inadvertently dumped the contents of my purse on the floor. Two kind lawyers got on their knees to help me pick up all the feminine articles that lay scattered under our feet and nearby chairs. Then with Caroline in my arms, I opened the courtroom door to face approximately three hundred pairs of eyes: all criminals just like me. At that moment, Caroline's *Sing Along Scripture Verse* book began to loudly play "Joshua Fought the Battle of Jericho." Wildly pushing buttons to try and get it to stop, I backed out of the courtroom, closed the door, and leaned against the wall weak with laughter. Caroline just grinned. When I composed myself and returned to the courtroom, the judge smiled kindly at me with a bemused expression. We celebrated that evening by making sugar cookies with pretty sprinkles and having a quiet little tea party.

Though I can now smile about those events, I have not forgotten the darkness that overwhelmed me at that time or the hope that I knew the Lord was extending to me. We see that failure can turn into a blessing in our lives as Brennan Manning says from *Lion and Lamb*. "Living out of the center has taught me that every failure succeeds in some way. It not only provides the opportunity to humble the self but to be gentle with the failures of others. If your life or mine were an untarnished success story, an unbroken spiral toward holiness, we might never come to understand the human heart." Facing these weaknesses in my life has only enhanced my understanding of His grace. I am well acquainted with my failures, but I am more aware of His unconditional love for me.

Though the Lord was redemptive to me that night and the days following, I am still walking in the aftermath of that chaos. I had a great deal of the expense with court costs as well as my insurance premium, which accelerated and will remain so for the next two years. Only the Lord can cause even Romans 8:28 to be true in this scenario, and He has caused good to come out of this story. For instance, for someone who used to receive speeding tickets on somewhat of a consistent basis, I haven't had a speeding ticket since that dark night. There have been other changes as well, though maybe not as obvious to others. I am aware of them as they all started on the inside.

Finding Balance

Whether we live as a lightning rod or spend uneventful days, how do we reach the middle of an impulsive life *versus* structured? Admittedly, I love the spontaneous personality that God gave me, but I am also aware of my need for Him to lead this wild and instantaneous nature of mine. Today God has guided me from a life that was totally out of control and into a lifestyle that is more yielded to His agenda rather than my own. No certificate hangs in my study of "Most Improved Chaos Queen"; however, I am now familiar with the quieter places in my heart.

Even my friends who are over-organized need these lessons. You see, the Holy Spirit desires that when He prompts us to do something we aren't pulling out a planner to see if we can fit Him in. We can deny the power and freedom of the Holy Spirit to move in our lives while living what we think is ordered godliness by being predictable. Proverbs 16:9 says, "A man plans his way but the Lord directs his steps." If we had respect and appreciation for the gift of time that has been given to us, our desire would be enhanced for His guidance in how we use our time. And if we choose to ignore His leading, there will always be the aftermath to deal with. This area is my little place of expertise and I will share some of my observations in my own life.

At times I have been tempted to blame my frustration and fatigue on other people. On many occasions my inability to say "no" to requests has sometimes caused me to see them as another source of stress. *"So many people to see or return calls. Is there no end? Aaaghh! I have literally been screaming on the inside. Please diffuse me Father, before I explode."* One of the reasons I enjoyed working in Labor and Delivery is because I got to be around women that could scream freely, something I have often wanted to do. If we reach a place where we are smiling on the outside yet resentful of individuals, it is a good time to have a heart and attitude assessment to examine the causes. Sharing the love of Christ with someone is different if we resent the time spent with them.

As far as organization goes, well, I will most likely never lead a seminar on it. However, from one who used to lose her planner at least three times a week, I can share some things that have helped me. Though they may seem like baby steps, they are at least in the right direction.

I invested in a *bigger* planner. I have had it for almost two years and have not lost it yet. My friend who *reeks* of organization spent about two hours guiding me on the practicalities of how to use this one in an optimum way. Granted, I was a month late on ordering my refill for this year; however, I have been encouraged to see the progress in this area.

How unfortunate that I wasn't using a planner when I arranged to meet a friend in California several years ago. In making arrangements to return from a class reunion in Oregon one year, I realized I had a layover in Los Angeles. *Too good to be true*, I thought. A wonderful guy with whom I had recently started corresponding lived in Los Angeles. So I called Butch and we set up a meeting at the airport. A few minutes before landing, I freshened my lipstick, put on some perfume, and looked out the window.

"Excuse me, sir," I said to the man on my right. "What is that massive bridge?"

"Why that's the Golden Gate Bridge!" he answered, amazed at my ignorance.

"But sir, the Golden Gate Bridge is in San Francisco," I said, confused.

"Lady, that's where we are landing," he answered, a little irritated.

Moaning, I fell back in my seat. I got the wrong city. Butch had driven an hour and a half through traffic to meet me and then waited as long at the airport. He ended up marrying a sweet girl named Susan who most likely is more organized than I and doesn't get major cities confused.

My family, who has always called me the "Bag Lady," was somewhat surprised at Christmas last year. All my life they have known to expect not only me for the holidays, but also my bags of unfinished, unbaked, and unwrapped gifts. Last year I gave them their presents on Christmas day. It is beside the point that I waited until they started opening some other gifts before passing out mine, since I needed their discarded gift bags. Thankfully, the labels came off with ease as I recycled them from behind the couch. The cross-stitch sampler for Brian, my brother-in-law, was not finished until the day after Christmas, but that was closer than any of my other handiwork gifts have been.

My mail and correspondence, however, are sadly in need of help. For example, my Christmas cards usually arrive in early spring. I still marvel that I actually mailed a letter to my good friends in Japan with pictures of my time in a Romanian orphanage. I felt strongly that I was to do this. Those pictures sparked something in the Kaylors' hearts despite the fact that they thought they had already completed their family. They began proceedings to adopt a child. When I see pictures of little Samuel, it is a reminder not to postpone taking time to write when we feel prompted.

Only in the last two years has my pastor encouraged me to create a mission statement for my life. He has seen me passionately run after so many things in the last ten years. They are all wonderful passions, but too much passion about everything can leave you tired. We can easily confuse all the things we enjoy for specific agendas the Lord has for us to be involved in. *"My natural talents and interests seem to lend themselves to obvious outlets. So much so that I don't think to pray about activities, actions, or opportunities before I plunge in. Sorry Lord, help me to rely on your leading."* And for single women, it is *not* our mission statement to be married but rather to streamline and clarify our natural talents and interests.

Though the process of change may be more gradual for some of us, we must not wait on perfection, but be open to God using us presently. As we visited over coffee recently, a friend described the hopelessness she felt in her desire to find balance and order in her life. I was reminded of a contrasting conversation with a beautiful single woman who seemed to live her life by an outline, yet was depressed because she felt uptight in her relationships. Yet another friend complained that she wanted to have other women into her home but was ashamed because her house was such a wreck all the time. "I don't want people to drop by and see me because I would be too embarrassed."

We know in our hearts the Lord does not require perfection of us, yet areas of practicality, such as keeping a clean home, are not unobtainable goals for most of us. Having an orderly home frees us to invite unexpected guests in while feeling comfortable. I know what it is like to try to keep a clean home when the swinging of my front door has had more action than my broom or mop. Keep in mind that our worth and value come from God's perspective and not other people's. And in the event that someone needs prayer and a time of listening while sitting on your couch and your house is a mess, toss your pride on one of the piles lying around and graciously invite them into your heart and home.

The Soul Place

Even broader than a mission statement, a planner, or a clean and ordered home is who we are in our souls when we are still. Are we a holy and quiet dwelling place for His presence? Perhaps your life reflects a previous place of my heart: *"As a still child may I rest my head against your heart because I am filled with unrestful thoughts. I feel as if I have lost touch with the pulse of God. I am living in the peripheral veins but not the main artery of Your life flow."* Upon recently discovering that journal entry, I was reminded of a portion of a verse that has become so precious to me from Zephaniah 3:17: "He will quiet you with His love." That verse has become interwoven into the fabric of my heart over the last three years. In the midst of some overwhelming circumstances, those out of my control as well as some that have been self-induced, God has consistently been quieting me with His love.

During this last year, I was introduced in concert to an eighth century Irish hymn that has become one of the themes of my life, "Be Thou My Vision." The words in themselves are reflective of the essence of our Christian walk. When anything begins to obscure our vision of God, we lose the clarity of our focus and will begin to falter and stumble. This song expresses my desire that He would be my vision above all other circumstances and in my daily desire to know Him more. Only when I spend time with Him can I maintain the focus of my vision.

But focus may be the tough part. How many times have I knelt to pray, write in my journal, or spend time in Scripture and the phone rings or I remember something that needs to be done? The thought occurred to me one day that if I was married and there was a little bit of romance going on, I would hardly interrupt such a time to catch the phone. If the dryer buzzed, I would certainly not jump up from an amorous encounter to deal with laundry. Not on your life! The thought is so ludicrous it makes me laugh! How could you possibly think of spoiling something so special by mere distractions? Yet, I find myself doing this all the time in my quiet time with the Lord. On countless occasions I have bounded from an intimate time of prayer and devotion to attend to trivial activities. Whenever we set aside time to spend with the Lord you can guarantee your life there will be interruptions. But consider these few spiritual events that have helped my focus to be on God.

Prayer. Years ago I read for the first time Richard Foster's *Celebration of Discipline.* Since that time I have short-circuited at least three snooze buttons from over usage in my desire to pray. Yet a great deal of my life has been spent in self-condemnation in my struggle to maintain a *structured daily* time with the Lord. With conflicting nursing sleep patterns and the quest to fill every waking moment with activities, it seemed I failed daily in this desire. Though I enjoyed many aspects of my relationship with the Lord, it has only been in the last couple of years that I stopped struggling and began *enjoying* my relationship with Him as never before.

If you are putting your devotional life on hold until a convenient time it most likely will never happen. There will never be enough time in your day to pray unless you make it. We may appear to be getting by on the fumes of some past experiences but eventually we will come to a sputtering halt—dry and empty. In my car, I have run out of gas more times than I care to remember because I didn't take time to stop for fuel—I even ran out twice in one day. I have done the same thing in my spiritual journey. Only when I have those daily times of prayer, study, and listening does my life stay on course with His will.

If your heart has struggled with prayer, ask the Lord to help you establish the daily discipline of time with Him. And when you would rather sleep than pray, as I often have, Oswald Chambers suggests that you, "Get up now and think about it later."

When working in Israel for a few months, I happened to be in walking distance of the Garden of Gethsemane. Remember that is where Jesus prayed all night while His disciples slept. I wanted to go and pray where Jesus did, and I did pray for a little while. It was so peaceful that I decided to lay down in the grass and meditate. Two hours later, I woke up from meditating. I did indeed feel terrible. I was no different than the disciples that we have all read about. Indeed, I am well acquainted with this struggle. Through this transition of enjoyment in my relationship with the Lord, I have been more aware of what I once heard referred to as a "posture of prayer." To me, this phrase has made me more attuned to an on-going conversation with Him and an awareness of His presence during the hours that I am not "formally praying."

As we become more familiar with Him, we will find that listening is as important as making requests. As quietness is cultivated, we learn to hear His voice with our hearts. When the Lord speaks to your heart, it is louder than any voice could speak to your ears. Ask freely and passionately with a heart full of faith. He *always* hears and answers our prayers though sometimes the answer is "no" which is as much of an answer as "yes." And sometimes our answers take more time than we want to give them and we can even suspect that He is not listening. I can't remember what I was frustrated about when I wrote: *"I sometimes wonder if I yelled and prayed louder that you would hear me."* He often delays purposely and the delay is just as much an answer to your prayer as the fulfillment when it comes. One of my most underlined verses is "For the vision is yet for the appointed time: It hastens toward the goal and it will not fail. Though it tarries, wait for it; it will certainly come, it will not delay" (Hab. 2:3).

Don't give up on the prayers that God has placed in your heart, and continue to seek Him with fervency and faith. We don't have to beg, whine, or plead. I have done them all. I have been amazed at how many "pleeeezes" I have found in my journal! When we pray, we certainly want to be careful to not just fill in the time praying for our needs and ourselves. "Greater love hath no man than this and that is to lay down his life for his friends" (John 15:13). I believe laying down our lives in prayer for those God has placed in our circle of influence is one of the greatest ways we can show love.

Retreat. Even though singles often live alone, we may not take the time to be alone and quiet with God. Sometimes we surround ourselves with activity and noise to fill in lonely voids or perhaps even because we are uncomfortable in solitude. On more than one occasion, I have literally thrown a backpack and sleeping bag into my car and headed off for a weekend of spiritual retreat under the stars just to regroup, ask for Gods mercy, and get away. Spiritual retreats for me have been as varied as a few hours or several days. Even a hike in the woods or an evening of turning the phone off can provide some uninterrupted time of renewal. In fact, it used to be easier for me to go away for a few days than to turn off the phone. For some, an evening without TV would be an act that would require sedation.

It's not practical to think of going away for a few days every time you need quiet, which is why the daily discipline of devotion and prayer is so important. But if you have never pulled away from people and activities for a period of time, I would encourage you to do so.

I am reminded of the words of Foster: "Solitude is inner-fulfillment. Solitude is not first a place but a state of mind and heart.... Therefore, we must seek out recreating stillness and solitude if we want to be with others meaningfully. We must seek the fellowship....Simply to refrain from talking without heart listening is not silence."

You don't have to head to the woods or remote places; however, I would encourage you to be open to specific times to pull away in a place beside your home. One of my greatest joys has been when friends have used my home as a retreat when I am away. Even something so simple as chapels provide wonderful opportunities to spend time alone. I am always exploring chapels whether those at airports or those I happen upon while traveling. I have had some meaningful quiet times in these little sanctuaries.

Fasting. In a world that tells us to pamper, coddle, and fill all of our inner-longings, fasting would hardly be considered vogue. Fasting takes the focus off of us and onto God. It puts us in a place of surrender to the physical dictates of our body. Every cell in your physical body will scream and demand to be fed. That is the problem, fasting is easy until you get hungry. You will feel like you are dying if you go for a few days without food and that is the good news...you will die to your own desires.

And if you ever want to go out for dinner just declare a fast! You will be amazed at the number of invitations you will receive or the number of people that will drop by with a special treat. It will make you laugh at Satan's creative attempts to entice you to indulge in a few tasty morsels.

This discipline is not a hunger strike, though I admit to having had a few of those. When I have fasted with the attitude of forcing God into answering prayer the only result has been hunger. Of course, the thought that I could actually force God into anything is so entirely ludicrous. Every cell in my body yells and whines and carries on like crazy when I say I am going to fast. Now understandably a day or so without food...but thirty minutes into a fast? After a while all the screaming hunger cells will cease and it has nothing to do with the coma you fear you might slip into at any moment. A fast does anything except go by fast but the eternal benefits are far beyond the sacrifice of temporary hunger.

Journaling. It is not required to keep a journal to get into heaven but it sure makes the journey sweeter. There have been so many times in my quietness and listening that I have taken up my journal to write as I hear the Lord speaking to me. My mind sometimes runs in so many directions at one time that I have a difficult time saying all I want to. The opportunity to write freely and uninterruptedly somehow sorts all those jumbled thoughts and brings clarity while tying them together. *From the beach: "A penny for my thoughts. I could be quite wealthy from my thoughts that are swirling, surrounding and multiplying in equations greater than this sand I love to walk upon. Yet Father, you know them from afar. Take these thoughts more tulmutuous than the ocean waves that you once walked upon and speak peace to them. For then they will be quiet and calm...glassy still. These same waters will be still and there I can see my reflection with yours mirrored behind me. In the chaos of the waves the reflection will be distorted but in the stillness I can see clearly."*

Katrine Stewart writes, "It is the human need to somehow keep a record of our lives. The more fragmented the life, the deeper the need. A journal is a book about our daily journey. It will never be completed. It will never be perfect. If you start your book with this in mind, you are already on a right path. Have courage to write about the little steps even

when they seem incoherent and haphazard. The rest will fall into place."
Not only does my journal provide a flow of thoughts and prayers, I can
sometimes see areas more clearly that I need Him to change. I couldn't
help but laugh at one rather revealing entry: "*The two young girls with
whom I am traveling with have never flown before; however, they have
taken a mothering role and are treating me like I am their child. Feeling
a little defiant, I told them I would take care of my own ticket. I turned
around and proceeded to almost fall on my face as I tripped on my backpack. Served me right. How nice to be in this position. Help me to be bigger than this, Father.*" At another time upon flying home from my first
trip into Russia, I was struggling with guilt about having nice and comfortable things. As I was praying, the Lord brought such clarity to me as
I wrote: "*Angela, it's not the things that are so important.*" As I was writing, it is as if I could see all of my earthly treasures in my hands though
they were open and flat. "*Your hand is to stay open around these things
Angela, never grasping or clutching them tightly. I am not requiring that
you give up "things" at present, but be grateful while you have them.*" In
my writing something was penetrating my heart in the midst of my
confusion and desire to know what my response should be. I realized
that when we start clutching at anything—whether in relationships or
possessions that make us feel secure—our heart of gratitude becomes
one of possessiveness, which is conflicting with humility and
gratefulness.

The last stirring words of *Be Thou My Vision* are the essence of
where our lives are going whether we realize it or not. One day He will
be all of our Vision as we stand in His presence. "Heart of my own heart,
whatever befall, Still be my vision, Oh ruler of all."

As we look at whatever chaos and disorder is in our lives inwardly
and outwardly, know that in our surrender to Him we will know the
truth of Isaiah 32:17: "And the effect of righteousness will be peace
(internal and external), and the result of righteousness will be quietness and confident trust forever." Though we are weak in areas we
desire to change, He loves us endearingly. Corrie Ten Boom tells of how
she learned of her heavenly Father's love through her own father. "When

as a child I couldn't sleep he would put his big hand over my little face. In prison, I would say to the Lord, 'Father, just put Your big hand over my little face.' Then I could sleep." Corrie's heart was stilled with the quietness and confidence that her Father was watching over her. I pray that you will know that same sweetness of His love for you as He becomes your Vision and permeates your life with His quietness and confidence.

Chapter Seven

STAMPING THE PASSPORT OF YOUR HEART

My eyes wandered slowly around the warehouse in Hong Kong. Thousands of Chinese Bibles were stacked neatly against the thick gray walls. A man began to give instructions for filling our backpacks with Bibles. He cautioned us not to pack more than we could carry, warning that we would have a long way to walk when we entered into China. Continuing with instructions for crossing the border, he warned us to walk alone and not with teammates. His closing remark was; "If you do get detained at the border, we will wait for you. They may confiscate your Bibles, but we do not think there will be any arrests. Do not give up your passport or divulge information about the ministry under any circumstances."

Our team was silent and sober. My youngest sister and I looked at each other and grinned. There was excitement in our hearts. We had never been overseas before, and here we were about to make our first trip into communist China. We had prayed for the Christians in the underground church for as long as I could remember.

Forgetting our leader's warning about going easy on the load, I began stuffing Bibles into my backpack. When not even one more page would fit, I buckled it and bent over to lift it onto my back. It felt like a midsize refrigerator, but I had come on this trip to get as many Bibles into China as I could, and I decided this was not a time to act prissy. I tugged and pulled the load over to a corner and sat on top of it exhausted. Pulling my favorite Scarlett O'Hara denial technique, I decided I would think about it later.

Later was in about five minutes when our team leader announced that it was time to leave. Dragging my backpack to the train which took us to the gates of the Chinese border, I started getting nervous, not about potential Chinese interrogation and torture, but about finding a good neurosurgeon who could speak English and perform emergency back surgery.

We all silently departed in separate directions, praying for the protection of each Bible that was about to cross into communist China. We had been told in our briefing not to appear nervous while going through customs, so as not to arouse the suspicion of the border guards. I was in too much pain to look nervous, but I knew if I dragged my backpack, someone might suspect that it held more than clothes.

Hoisting it onto a bench, I somehow managed to maneuver it onto my back. When I stood upright, my chest was extended several inches and I could feel my shoulder blades touching. I knew that if I leaned forward I was going to topple onto my head. All of this time I was praying, "Oh God! You have got to help me look inconspicuous." I knew I had the sure markings of an overzealous first time Bible smuggler, and they were going to yank me in for questioning the minute they saw me.

My mind racing, I concluded that "tourist incognito" was my best shot. Stuffing three pieces of bubble gum into my mouth, and putting on my sunglasses, I swung my camera around my neck and put my baseball cap on backwards. Then I picked up a Chinese magazine from a nearby garbage can, careful not to lean forward and land on my head. I was going to be an obnoxious American tourist and a good one at that. Smacking on my big wad of gum, blowing *big* bubbles, and swinging my hips in rhythm to my gum smacking, I sauntered toward customs. As I intently "read" my Chinese magazine, I did not look to the right or left at the many officials but concentrated on keeping my shoulders up, blowing bubbles, and reading while rhythmically swinging my hips. Seeing the team on the other side and realizing I had successfully cleared customs was one of the most exhilarating moments of my life.

Several from our team had been stopped, including my sister, and I was convinced it was my obnoxious behavior that had gotten me through. On occasion, I have found that the art of being obnoxious can be very useful. I had some help getting my backpack off my shoulders, and I suspected my clavicles were permanently hyperextended. Walking along a narrow dirt path that led to a country village, we deposited our treasures in a secured and empty building. We had completed the first leg of the journey, getting the Bibles past the border. Now the Chinese Christians would pick them up and take them to believers in the underground church. It was sobering and humbling to leave the Bibles in the little obscure building, knowing they were going deep into the interior of China.

We made daily trips into China, and I eventually adjusted to the idea that I could not carry quite as many Bibles as a pack mule. I lightened up my load a little, but the burden in my heart grew heavier for those believers who didn't have a Bible, as well as for the millions of unbelievers in Asia and other parts of the world.

On the plane home, I reflected deeply upon what had taken place in my heart and thanked God for enlarging my vision and helping me to see beyond my own little world. I knew my life would never be the same. Not only would there be many more trips overseas, but there would also be a new awareness of hurting and lost souls around me. I had finally begun to see what my pastor and his wife had been telling me for years: God loved the world—both near to and far from me—and He wanted to use me to touch it.

Beyond Ourselves

Certainly the Lord wants us as His children to walk in pleasures that He has intended for us. Solomon made mention of this desire in Ecclesiastes 5:18: "It is good [for man] to enjoy the days of life that God gives him; this is the gift of God." But when that pleasure becomes self-centered, it ultimately loses its savor.

What are we investing our lives in as single women? The pursuit of a husband? Our careers? Our homes? Entertainment? Our society promotes self-centeredness, placing an emphasis on individual fulfillment at all costs, and even we Christians have embraced the idea that our time and resources are our own. We must learn to see our lives and blessings as gifts to treasure and *give freely*. When we do, I believe we will find greater fulfillment than we have ever known.

First, we must come to a place of gratefulness for God's deep and passionate love toward us. When we do, we will live a life that extends beyond ourselves to the hearts and lives of others. Our goals and the way we live our lives will change—even how we spend our time and money. After all, if those things belong to God, we need to get His guidance on how to use them. If you are like I am, this mindset will take some getting used to. Though ashamed to admit it, I have struggled as much as anyone with what James Twitchell has called our national religion: shopping. In his book, *Lead Us into Temptation,* Twitchell addresses one of the facts of life for our modern culture: that shopping and the accumulation of possessions is the way the vast majority of Americans search for contentment, fulfillment, and meaning.

Not long ago, I faced a crossroad in my desire for things. I found the most beautiful runner at a little specialty shop near my home. For days and days, I thought about buying it. I went to admire it again, and the sales staff encouraged me to take it to my home to see how it would look. As I gazed approvingly at the lovely rug on my living room floor, I heard a National Public Radio update on Kosovo. The newscaster was describing such horrible atrocities against the Albanian women and children who were being dragged from their homes and raped. I can't describe how shallow and even nauseated I felt to think of women like me being subjected to such torment. Silently, I rolled up the rug and drove back to the shop. Shortly thereafter, I began sponsoring a pair of Albanian children through a Christian relief organization. Instead of a rug, I now look at and pray for two adorable, precious faces on my refrigerator.

The decision to which that radio broadcast pushed me involved more than my money: it also made me face the fact that my desire for material possessions had superceded my awareness of others' needs.

I had lost my focus on the reality of eternity and had become susceptible to a serious, life-threatening disease called *People Blindness*. This
malady attacks us when we build up immunity to the needs around us.
Changing our focus and placing it on eternal issues is never easy. But as
we are busy about our Father's business and not just about our own
concerns, God will take our hearts and fill them with His tenderness
and compassion.

Look around you, nearby at first, for the opportunities God has
placed in your path. The problem is not in finding an area to be involved
in; it's a matter of choosing in which opportunity to be an expression of
Him and light in darkness. I once heard someone say, "God wants to
walk around in our bodies." Perhaps He wants to walk through you to
other countries or through the doors of an inner-city ministry or a crisis pregnancy center. If you have been going to Bible studies all your
life, could this be the time that you lead one? Without question, some of
the highlights of my adult life have been the wonderful life-changing
times when God has opened my eyes to people who need me. Often,
they have been near me—in my church, neighborhood, or even my
own family—though some have been thousands of miles away.

Seeing People with His Eyes
Recently, the Lord allowed me to experience two personal word pictures
concerning People Blindness in my own life. While shopping for spring
flowers at my favorite garden shop, I spotted a delightful children's
swing. It was weathered and charming and tucked away in an unobtru-
sive corner as if waiting for me to discover it. When I inquired about the
price, I was thrilled and was already envisioning my nieces and little
friends swinging in it. Since I know the gentleman who owns the shop,
I asked him to hold my discovery for a few minutes while I drove home
for my checkbook. Unfortunately, once home I allowed myself to get
sidetracked until after the shop had closed that afternoon. When I went
back the next day to purchase my very special swing, it was gone. My
heart sank, and I berated myself for my missed opportunity.

A similar situation arose a few months later. On a country road near my home, I had discovered an old, neglected one-room chapel in a field surrounded by weeds. For six years I had driven by this winsome structure and had been drawn to its solitude and beauty. Finally one day I decided to approach the owners of this land and ask about purchasing the chapel and having it moved. As I approached the property that day, I was horrified. My quaint little prayer chapel had been pushed into a pile of rubble and an aluminum house put in its place.

For many days afterwards, I thought about these missed opportunities and had a sinking sensation. Then as I prayed for God to teach me something from them, I distinctly heard the Lord say, "Angela, I want you to see people as that swing and the little church. The times that you have put off sharing or waited for a better moment have ended just like this. Just as these material opportunities are gone, so are some of the opportunities I have given you with people. Only people are eternal, and the church building and swing, as wonderful as they were, are not."

Often we fail to seize an opportunity to minister to someone, because we think we will have another chance. But sometimes we simply fail to recognize another person's value in His sight. Some of the things in my home that guests have complimented me on the most are the things I have picked up as others' discards. But over the years I have developed an eye for these little treasures, looking beyond the scars and blemishes and seeing the potential. And we must all learn to develop that eye with people too. God forbid that we ever look upon people as human discards—rancid and nasty garbage. It is so easy to be critical and irritated, but when we see others through His eyes, we will feel the Father's compassion for His needy children. On those occasions when my judgmental heart finally got out of the way, I felt the compassionate heartbeat of God pulsing through my life. At those moments my heart agrees with the words of Brennan Manning from *Lion and Lamb*: "We are never more like Jesus than when we are choked with compassion. I pray you have the courage to set free the song that now sleeps in the wounded flesh of a brother or sister." We will only be able to hear God's compassionate heartbeat as we stay near to His heart.

Perhaps one of the greatest hindrances to seizing opportunities to share with others is the feeling of inadequacy. We may acknowledge the needs around us but feel unqualified to meet them. For years, I fell into this category. Even though I had become a Christian at an early age, I didn't think I knew the Scriptures pertaining to salvation well enough to be able to share them. I finally enrolled in an evangelism course that forced me to learn Scriptures, an outline, and some wonderful word pictures.

Since I am not an outline kind of girl, getting through the course was challenging for me. The first time my partner and I went out to share, I felt like a disaster waiting to happen. I just knew I would slip up on the basic two introductory questions and say something like, "Who am I and what am I doing here?" When the first woman I witnessed to actually wanted to pray to receive Christ, I was so shaken up that I almost talked her out of it. I'm sure my partner was doing double time in prayer! The following Christmas I saw her ringing the Salvation Army bell and was thrilled to learn that she had gotten involved in a wonderful inner-city church and was being discipled.

We are *all* called to go into all the world and preach the gospel to the needy souls around us. If you lack confidence in this area, let me encourage you to take a course like I did. And, by all means, pray for those who are lost and hurting both across the street and across the ocean. Perhaps the most important aspect of mission work is prayer. Even without having a passport stamped, we can touch other parts of the world by getting on our knees. I use a prayer journal that highlights different countries for every day of the year and gives statistics about each population group. Praying for other nations, as well as for those around us, softens our hearts and broadens our vision beyond ourselves. It's humbling to think that some of the people for whom we pray may have no one else to pray for them.

As we prepare to share our faith, we must also choose to set aside our fears and pride and be sensitive to the Holy Spirit. A number of years ago, I had to make this choice. Strolling down a little side street in the Old City of Jerusalem, I was drawn into a small and quaint art gallery.

Eli Schwartz, the owner and artist, was sitting behind his counter and did not appear friendly. I smiled at him anyway and spent the next thirty minutes or so browsing among his interesting works. His painting of a gnarled and twisted Menorah especially caught my attention, and I stood silently, studying it for a long while.

"Sir, would you please tell me the symbolism of this painting?" I asked. His response shocked me and he seemed offended by the question. With much gesticulating and dramatic gusto, he began a tirade on the improprieties of asking an artist to interpret his work. I was taken aback by his reaction and turned to walk out the door. Suddenly I felt that I should go back and have a conversation with him, despite his gruff demeanor.

Taking a deep breath and plunging in I said, "Sir, you have hurt my feelings by your response to my question. I am sorry I have offended you but I only wanted to know what that painting meant to you, the creator."

He looked surprised and almost amused. "Well now!" he said. "Come and sit down and I will talk to you about the painting." An hour later we were still in conversation, and I was delighted at the turn of events. My new friend Eli was asking me questions about Christianity, and I was prayerfully asking guidance for my responses to him. He did not embrace the gospel that day but he did hear it. When I left his gallery, I thanked God for helping me to be more sensitive to His Holy Spirit than to my own offended pride.

A few years later, I faced a similar choice in the Ukraine. For several days, I had been lecturing to more than a hundred nursing students on the psychological aspects of nursing. One evening, as I looked over my notes for the next day's talk, I felt a strong burden in my heart for the souls of these young women. Knowing that my host college might frown on a gospel presentation, I decided to meet this burden by sending the girls nursing penlights and Christian tracts after my return to the US. The next morning, however, I could not shake the sense of urgency that the Holy Spirit had placed within me. During devotions, I turned to one of our team members and asked him to pray for me. I felt completely immersed in fear and panic. He reminded me that Jesus cultivated godly dependence in His disciples by putting them in situations in which they desperately needed Him. I was an excellent candidate. An hour later, I stood in front of the class filled with confidence—not in myself but in God—and shared the gospel with these students. Three fourths of them raised their hands to make a commitment to Christ. My teammate and I were thrilled as we prayed with them and arranged for Ukrainain Christians to follow up with these students. If I had shared that day out of the strength of my personality or confidence in my ability, I am afraid to say what might have happened. Remember that as you step out in faith to do whatever God has entrusted to you, let your confidence be in Him and be assured He will not fail you.

Even the Ordinary

My experiences in Jerusalem and in the Ukraine—like my trip into China—were thrilling, to say the least. But unfortunately, we often think more of sensational events than ordinary ones. What would be considered one of the more important events of my life, the excitement of smuggling Bibles into a communist country, or cooking a meal for an international family with a new baby? As a friend has said, "If we can't walk out of our front door and love our neighbor, why go to another country to do the same?" I am thankful to have had the opportunity to travel extensively, but most of my contacts with other people occur during my daily routine at home, in my neighborhood, and at work.

Leo Tolstoy addresses this issue in his wonderful short story, *Where There is Love, There is God.* Tolstoy tells a rich parable of the old carpenter Avdyeitch who spends an entire day waiting for the Lord to visit him so that he might show God his devotion. Instead, needy people pass the carpenter's way all day. Avdyeitch gives freely to them but at the end of the day is disappointed that the Lord never came. At that moment the Lord appears to the old man and says, "Did you not recognize Me? I was hungry and you fed Me. I was thirsty and you gave Me drink. I was cold and you clothed Me. In as much as you have done it to the least of these, you have done it unto Me." We sometimes miss the simple, quiet opportunities to minister to Him, while waiting for something big and spectacular.

Often some of the most precious opportunities for true ministry can be in our own families. Because my parents divorced when I was very young and my mother remarried during my early childhood, my stepfather has virtually always been my primary father figure. As is the case for most fathers and daughters, my early and teenage years presented us with some challenges to love and forgive as we struggled in the journey to know each other. But we met these challenges and grew in mutual appreciation.

My adult years with Dad have been especially sweet. My journey with him during the last year of his life—from the day he was diagnosed with cancer to the day he died—was one of the most bitter yet precious experiences I've ever known. Over a period of several months, I accompanied Dad to the oncologist for chemotherapy and radiation treatments. I watched him suffer terribly and become very ill. During his last week in the hospital, the care I provided for him stretched me beyond anything that had ever been required of me as a nurse. Yes, I had performed those same duties for other girls' fathers, but never for my own. I had never faced such darkness and overwhelming grief. But the Lord gave me the courage, grace, and tenderness to care for Dad. I will always be grateful for this opportunity, which I am sure ranks every bit as special in God's heart as smuggling Bibles into China.

We would never choose to see our loved ones suffer, yet it can so easily be part of our lives in a fallen world, especially as we and our parents get older. Disease—both physical and mental—problems in interpersonal relationships, business failures, moral violations, and heartbreak may plague members of your family who need your support. In this event, embrace the chance to love and serve your loved ones as unto the Lord, not as a lesser ministry but as a high calling.

Our neighborhoods also provide multiple opportunities to share the love of the Father. Smiling, taking time to talk to the children, welcoming new babies and new neighbors, getting the newspaper for the elderly, and baking chocolate chip cookies are just some of the ways to show you care. And you never know how the Lord might use one of these neighborly gestures.

A new guy moved in next door to me a little over a year ago. Right away, I wanted to bake him something. And no, not just because he was single. I almost didn't get around to it. Trips out of town, a hectic work schedule, and family concerns seriously limited my time at home, and I nearly decided a welcome-to-the-neighborhood goody would seem more embarrassingly late than delicious. Putting aside pride, however, I presented him with a fresh baked chocolate cheesecake exactly three hundred sixty-four days after he arrived, barely making my favorite Emily Post one-year etiquette rule! As always, God had a way of redeeming the time; my new neighbor was right in the middle of stressful law school finals and welcomed prayer and cheesecake. I felt as if I was right on schedule.

Unless you are independently wealthy, you most likely have a job, which means you are probably working with people who are not Christians. Pray for those you are working with. And be aware of opportunities to share with those around you through love and kindness. Perhaps your peers are walking through difficult situations and need your support and encouragement. Over a seven-year period, I had the opportunity to work with a group of girls who really were like a big group of sisters. Despite all the hormonal tensions typically associated with women who work together, we felt deep loyalty and commitment to each other. Some of us had times of prayer for one another, and I kept my own list of their prayer needs. They certainly knew I wasn't perfect or saintly, but they trusted me and knew that I loved them. You don't need to stand on a desk and share the four points of salvation; consistent love and prayer will touch their hearts far deeper than just words.

"Preach the gospel at all times. If necessary use words."
—*Francis of Assisi*

Being connected and part of a church family opens a wide and wonderful door to give of yourself. From leading a Bible study, keeping the nursery, working with children's church, arranging flowers, and helping with the internationals, to visiting the elderly, helping with the tape ministry, or filling communion cups. The list goes on forever and may include some items that church committees never thought of.

I met a young girl through a mutual friend. She became part of a Bible study in my home and started visiting my church. She lived in Birmingham, without her family, and was planning her wedding, which she would pay for herself. I encouraged them to use my pastor for pre-marital counseling, and to help her out, I volunteered to direct her wedding. Had I ever directed a wedding? *No.* Nor had I ever decorated a barn for a wedding reception. Martha Stewart would have been impressed with my results, though, I am sure. Despite the fact that our hundreds of narcissus bulbs bloomed a week too early, my dress kept flying open because I ran out of time to sew on the buttons, and the flower girl was out of control, my friend had a lovely wedding and reception and is living happily ever after. I had just wanted to help and ended up enjoying it as much as she did. Well, maybe not *quite* as much!

Children's ministries, both within and outside of our churches, give us an excellent chance to nurture the little ones for whom Jesus has a special love. The simple act of showing a child that someone cares can change his or her young life. A number of community programs can connect you with a child who needs someone. I have friends who have developed wonderful relationships with children they've reached out to in literacy/tutoring programs, or in ways as simple as a weekly phone call, a trip to the ice cream parlor, a day in the park, or a trip to the library. As you mentor and show Christ's love to a child, you can help her set goals, provide an increased sense of belonging and security, and encourage better performance in school. I recently read a caption that caught the attention of my heart: "Changing the World...One Child at a Time." Smile at children and hug them whenever you can. We can never appreciate the eternal impact we can have upon their impressionable young lives or how they can touch ours.

Fulfilling the mandate of Jesus, "Go ye into all the world and preach the gospel," has never been so easy. The *world* has literally come to us.

Any major university campus usually has at least seventy nations represented by students that are generally in the top five percent of their nation academically. Nonetheless, they often face loneliness, homesickness, and fear of the unknown here in America. Many churches and campus ministries have outreaches to internationals and offer Friendship/Partner programs. Get involved; even if you never leave your hometown, you can "go into all the world" by being a friend. These students are hungry for friendships and conversation. When the word gets around that your home is available, all you have to do is open the door.

Of course, as single women we should exercise caution and wisdom, especially with international males from countries where women do not spend time alone with men. Be sensitive to customs and norms and when necessary, organize group activities. On the other hand, our impact on the women can be dramatic. An Iranian Christian man recently made a statement to Larry Lutz, international coordinator for the AD 2000 Women's Track: "The way to win the Muslims to Christ is through the women," he said. "They have the strongest influence on their sons! But it will take women to reach Muslim women." As women, we have an incredible opportunity to make an eternal impact upon the millions of Muslims and other internationals that have come to the United States.

All around us, in the most unexpected places, there are people with tremendous needs. Find out what is available and needed in your community or sign up for an outreach in another city or region. My life has been enriched by friends who are pouring their lives into ministries that I am not involved in, but love to hear about. We can't be a part of every opportunity, but we can effectively be a part of something and make a difference. The possibilities are limitless: teaching an adult to read, working with special needs children and adults, helping alcoholics and the homeless.

A couple of years ago I was in Philadelphia on a medical outreach. The experience changed me forever. While having coffee at a quaint street cafe one morning, I met a delicate, frail young woman. She smiled at me. Soon we were talking and having coffee and muffins together.

With regret and shame, she told me the story of her past as a prostitute; then she shared about her recent diagnosis of breast cancer and her fear not only for her own life but also for her daughter's. She wasn't asking for help, yet I wanted to be a part of her life. I knew of some assistance programs our medical team could connect her with and asked if she would meet me the next day. Again we had coffee and bagels and talked. I gave her information that I hoped would help her, as well as some money. I told her about Jesus as we walked to a park and wept together at the realization of His love. Although our backgrounds and colors were so different, we found a common bond in Christ. There was a humility and gratefulness in her heart that provoked me to want the same. That sweet girl put her head in my lap as I prayed for her and stroked her hair. I am sure we were a curious blend, and I felt the stares of busy people hurriedly passing by. Somehow, though, it seemed so natural and wonderful. And it was—two daughters in the embrace of their Father.

Involved in a Nation

Who would have ever dreamed that our nation would be in the state of decay and degradation that we have succumbed to? In listening to the news it almost seems surreal and like a bad dream. Where were Christians when decisions were made in our legislative and judicial branches of government that are so blatantly contrary to our nations biblical foundation? As Christians, we should be citizens who seek to influence the nation in which we have been blessed to live. Don't hesitate to stand up politically for what is true and right and godly. Pray with diligence for our leaders as the Bible encourages us to do. The decisions being made by them and by you will affect the moral and spiritual climate of our country for years to come. We cannot take the liberty of shaking our head and turning away in despair or disgust. Our involvement in the political process is essential, if we desire to see change. Pray above all, and then seize opportunities to make an impact.

One of the most important moral issues facing our nation is that of abortion. A couple of years ago, my friend Karen visited me from Israel.

While traveling together we listened to the news. Hearing an update on partial-birth abortion, she turned to me and asked me what this procedure involved. She had lived in Israel for several years and was not familiar with this recent "medical breakthrough." When I described it in simple terms, her eyes widened and she exclaimed in horror, "My God! I can't believe what I am hearing." I was reassured by her reaction, since I often feel as if the rest of the Christian world is far too complacent in the midst of our "American holocaust." Endangered unborn babies *and* their mothers need us to reach out to them. And as single Christian women, we can have a unique and powerful voice in this debate. Hundreds of crisis pregnancy centers all over the United States need volunteers in every capacity: promoting abstinence among youth, counseling pregnant or post-abortive women, opening our homes to unwed mothers, giving financial support. The possibilities for outreach in this area are endless. I honestly believe that when we feed, give drink to, and clothe the most defenseless members of our culture—the unborn— we, like Tolstoy's old carpenter Avdyeitch, are doing it unto the Lord.

Of course, sometimes we lose sight of the fact that we're doing things as unto the Lord, and situations don't quite work out the way we'd like for them to. Be careful not to claim you are filled with "righteous indignation" when it is really just your sinful response of anger. On more than one such occasion in my life, the old halo has toppled off my saintly head and landed with a "clunk." Once I felt I should give some money to a homeless person, who had only one leg. As he hobbled toward my car, the light changed, and this GQ kind of guy, sitting in a shiny BMW behind me, began honking his horn. I was *so* angry I wanted to crunch his pretty little car. Pulling up next to him at the next light, I yelled out, "You idiot! Did you expect he could *run* to me?" I was outraged. "You ought to be ashamed," I said scathingly, giving him the most condescending look I could muster, and I pulled away fuming. In a period of a few minutes, I had been transformed from Mother Teresa to someone who should fly away on a broom. I am not as consistent as I need to be. These are the sort of reactions that remind me that I need a Savior daily.

147

Across the Seas

Some of you may not feel called to cross the ocean. But it's kind of like tasting *creme brûlé* after years of instant vanilla pudding; you will never know how delectable it is until you try it. My first trip overseas— to China in 1988—opened not only my eyes but my heart to the world. My life was changed forever as I took a first real glimpse beyond myself. Since then I have taken advantage of every opportunity I could squeeze into my schedule and budget to travel overseas in ministry opportunities. Each experience has made an incredible impact on my life. As I have gone with the desire to serve and give, I found that I received *so* much more than I gave.

Whether it has been working with young girls at a Russian camp, or helping with physical assessments at a Romanian orphanage, my journals are filled with testimonies of answered prayers. Tender stories remind me of God's faithfulness to His children all over the world. Memories make me smile as I recall the many moments of laughter. I'm not saying that I have not been stretched at times! Trekking through Guyana's mud in a skirt and Birkenstocks under the blazing sun was a tough one for me. As I passed goats and cows along the path, I couldn't tell who smelled worse, them or me. But I would go back to that wonderful country if given the opportunity. My heart blended with those precious, beautiful people as we had a significant time of outreach in their village.

It's always a challenge for me to get myself together for one of these trips. I usually feel like I need to rededicate my life by the time I board the plane. But all the effort and hard work is slight in comparison with the wonderful events that take place. Perhaps you are wondering about the finances for all of these travels. Well, at times I have as well! The finances have always been provided, though sometimes at the last minute and on occasion the day after. I suppose since the Lord knows of my struggle with promptness, He figures a day late will be okay. Whatever! If the Lord knocks on the door of your heart to go overseas, He will provide. It may be through an extra job as I have done or in some other unexpected way.

Are you ready to switch from the instant vanilla pudding of life and plunge headfirst into some *creme brûelé*?! Or is your mouth watering but you are afraid to take your first bite? If you have never traveled outside of your comfort zone other than for pleasure, most assuredly you will have thoughts concerning your safety. There are no guarantees except that there is no safer place to be than in His will. *Please* don't let fear stop you, for His perfect love will cast out fear. If you don't have peace in your heart about an opportunity, that is entirely different. The Lord will confirm His direction for you by wise counsel, His Word, His voice, and His peace.

I knew the Lord had specifically told me to go to Israel although I was unsure of the timing. Wouldn't you know that the time He opened up was in the fall of 1991. To refresh your memory, that was just as all the Gulf War events were about to get started. There is nothing like sending me, "the lightning rod," to a war zone. I arrived in Jerusalem to work in a Christian ministry where people from all over the world came to pray for Israel and world events. I felt it was such a great privilege to be in that nation at such a critical time. Not only for the significance of praying but for the countless opportunities I had to share with those that were afraid. Not to mention I was having a wonderful time and felt a great deal of peace. A journal entry indicates a slight change of heart as the emotional climate intensified. "*We had our first discussion last night on preparing for possible war. For the first time I felt genuine fear. I don't mind dying if it is the Lord's will but otherwise I can't say I'm wild about a needless demise. This is too incredible to be sitting here in Jerusalem waiting for a gas mask. Is this a memory or what?*" It was just a matter of days before another benchmark time took place in the nation of Israel and once again all eyes of the world were upon her.

I was awakened that night to the pounding on my door with the announcement that Tel Aviv had been attacked. The sounds of angry shouting and sirens filled the air and people were frantically running by our windows. My sister Shawn called while I was still struggling to get dressed. She was in Japan and had just seen the news and was now crying with fear that I was about to be obliterated. The rest of the world knew about the war while I was still sleeping. And now here I was still trying to wake up. I calmly reassessed the situation after I had some coffee.

There I was in the middle of the Gulf War and having the time of my life. I was happy when all outgoing flights were cancelled. I was even enjoying the alarms in the middle of the night when all of our guests and staff entered into the two sealed rooms in the basement that we called "The Ark." Fortunately my bedroom was one of the rooms so I never had to run far if the sirens sounded in the middle of the night. If they went off in the middle of the day I grabbed all the important items like children and the coffeepot and joined everyone else. You never knew when the alarms would sound off so it was always important to have your gas mask with you. Only once did I forget mine and discovered its absence when I was at the market. I quickly made preparations to get back to the Mount of Olives where I stayed, but was eyeing a pile of eggplants that I would bury my head in if the alarm sounded before I got out of there.

I enjoyed my experience there immensely. Even the day some of the boys on the mountain decided to take a free-for-all with rocks as I was walking had it's highlight. Several hours later while I was having stitches in my head, I was laughing with my Arab doctor (whom I believe was beginning to think I had neuro damage) and was able to share about the joy and peace of the Lord.

I share that experience to illustrate that we can't make decisions based on our own natural understanding or feelings but on His leading and guidance. I don't have the time to say all the wonderful things that happened during my time there, but how thankful I am that I listened to God's prompting to go. It made no sense intellectually to head to the Middle East when discussions of a war were taking place. It is a matter of being called, obeying, and watching Him take care of the details.

Another example was to follow a few years later. When my friends first asked me to take care of their children in a closed Muslim country while they were in language school, I didn't even know where the country was. Soon, though, I was on my way and in for some real treats.

I chronicled my time there in letters home, which I labeled *The Lopland Governess Reports*. They paint a fairly accurate picture of the delectable experience—the *creme brûlé*—which an opportunity overseas can provide. I wanted to share the first week with you for a glimpse of transcontinental life as it happened in our little spot of this Big World. (The reason you have never heard of Lopland is because it is a creative way of protecting the identity of my friends and their mission work there.)

The Lopland Governess Report: Week One

"Things are well. So far, the boys have only had to put me in time-out three times and just one spanking. I think they are pleased that I am so easy to manage. My little charges are Bill, Jim, Steve, and Adam, four little personalities who make me laugh a lot, not to mention a few other emotions. Curious George has become one of my favorite books, though it makes me a little nervous that one of the boys is going to get some ideas. Tonight as I read about Curious George getting in trouble, I subtly added a line about his "time-out" from the man with the yellow hat. It didn't work, for Jim informed me that I wasn't reading it correctly.

"Life here is full in the land of Lop but very nice to be a part of. I'm keeping a record of how many times a glass can be spilled during one meal. I think there may be a potential Guinness. We have had a problem with mice but fortunately not possums. Yesterday the boys and I caught one with Russell Stover candy in seven minutes flat after we loaded the trap. I think I gained tremendous ground in the boys' respect for my authority after such an awesome feat, even though I had just danced around the kitchen howling after pinching my finger in the trap.

"My flights over were good and I had a very nice visit in London with friends. As I got ready to board, I was informed that I would have to pay $150 for Lillie's and Bob's extra luggage that I was bringing. Since I had already paid over $100 in Birmingham, I just didn't think it was worth it for them to have a suitcase full of chocolate chips, brown sugar, and other baking ingredients. I spread out all the loot in an area of the London airport and tried to fit the contents of three suitcases into two. I took out the

inner-plastic bags of sugar and brownie mixes, and wildly tossed their cardboard boxes into the garbage, upsetting the little cleaning lady who kept having to empty the trash. Doing anything I could to lighten the load, I stuffed my coat pockets with brown sugar, thinking I would just wear the bags onto the plane. But when I put my coat on, I looked as if I had two huge goiters on my hips. Well, for those of you who know how I am about these hips, four bags of brown sugar got reduced to one bag of chocolate chips. I offered the ticket agent the extra suitcase and brown sugar if he would reduce the charge, and he lowered it to $50. Not bad in exchange for the happy little faces I would see as those four little guys were tearing into the suitcases and opening their treats from friends and grandparents from home. I guess even that thirty-pound waffle iron was worth it. I was very tempted to use it in my bartering with the ticket agent, but since the Loploodles love waffles on Saturday, I suppose the herniated disc was a small price to pay.

"The weather has been very pleasant, briskly cold outside and warm inside. I'm still getting used to the dress code. If I have sweats on in the house, I have to throw a skirt over them to go out with the boys or if someone comes in. These are the minors of being in a new culture. I wish I could speak their language. I met two sweet teenage girls yesterday when I was out strolling Adam. I so wanted to be able to speak with them. We just smiled at each other and tried to piece words together.

"A quick mention of the food: we have the most delicious apricots and dates I have ever tasted and fresh yogurt that gets delivered in the neighborhood. They are real treats for me, simple and delightful pleasures.

"Just a few thoughts about my week: it's Friday and since I don't have a date tonight, I have encouraged Bob and Lillie to go out. It won't be a romantic evening for me but certainly a fun one. Not just one man in my life but four little ones!

Signing off with love, The Gov"

By the end of my second week there, I was having a blast and dreading coming home.

The Lopland Governess Report: Week Two

"The lights just went out and it seemed like a nice time to catch up on my journal by candlelight. Fortunately, four little boys are asleep so there is no danger of being torched. The only negative part of this evening is that I am missing my favorite Lop cooking show. Low fat is out here, and plump is in. This is not good for a governess figure, as all good governesses should look regal and not portly. After I am finished with my governess position, I would like to return as the next Julia Child of Lopland.

"However, if I do return to start my own cooking show, I believe I will indulge in the luxury of having someone do my shopping, but it won't be Steve. He is an amazing child. I am still fascinated by his ability to stumble and fall when he isn't moving, to flip upside down when he was just sitting upright, and to spill something from a container that is empty. On our venture to buy eggs this week, he, Adam, and I set out for a local market with our little egg pail. Shopping is indeed an unpredictable adventure here and you must be prepared to visit several stores for a basic item. If you can't be flexible and patient, for the sake of your psychological safety you should stay home and fast. Fortunately, nice brown eggs are plentiful at a nearby market, probably because the neighborhood roosters who wake us up each day must have plenty of girlfriends in this neighborhood. On this particular morning after our egg purchase, I asked Steve to hold the pail while I strapped Adam into his stroller. Yes, I should have known better. Eggs that have fallen on a concrete floor look the same here as they do in America. Every time we go into this store now, the shopkeepers break into big smiles and I know they are wondering what we are going to do this time for entertainment. I don't think we have ever disappointed them.

"On another outing for soap detergent this week we finally found some in the one-room hardware store. Well, of course, whom should we run into but the milk lady? She was so excited to see us and was wildly talking and gesturing as if I really knew a word of what she was saying. Somehow she made her point and I left the hardware store not only with soap but also with two open jars of yogurt and cream. No lids. Managing them

carefully as I strolled Adam and held Steve's hand, I made one final stop at the bakery (a small room where flattened dough is slapped against the ancient stone wall where it sticks until baked and removed with a wooden pole) to buy the round flat Lop bread that you buy fresh everyday.

"As the boys and I were about to enter the bakery, I noticed that people were looking at us even more than usual. I knew it was about to turn into one of those Lucille Ball kind of days when I saw a group of women sweeping the street and motioning as if to say we were getting their street dirty. They were pointing to my dress. Looking down I saw that the whole front of my jumper was covered in cream and I was dripping yogurt. Puddles at my feet, we started a very rapid walk home.

"Now Adam is an all-terrain kind of little fellow. The more potholes you hit with his stroller, the happier he is. He was having a big time as we were careening around corners with yogurt oozing from my boots. Steve had been running beside us trying to keep up. Suddenly I felt a weight on the stroller and noticed that he had decided to hold on, slowing down my effort to end this shopping saga as quickly as possible. 'Steve, **why** are you pulling instead of pushing?' Looking up with his incredible brown eyes, he solemnly answered, 'cause, cause I just wanna be near you.' At that moment, I realized that there really are more terrible things in life than dairy products running down my legs, and one would be missing a leisurely stroll home with this sweet little boy holding my hand. Of course, I'm sure Adam was disappointed at our slowed pace.

"After we got home, I peeled off my clothes at the door and was about to change, when I heard Steve yelling from the outside toilet that he needed tissue, the phone ringing, and the milk lady banging on the gate. (I guess she had seen our trail.) I went flying to the other end of the house in my very non-traditional Lop attire to get the phone. Of course, it stopped ringing as soon as I got my hand on it. Lillie has a saying that seemed appropriate at the moment. 'If you can laugh about it later, you can laugh about it now.' And so with Steve yelling and the milk lady banging, I laughed aloud and life was good. A day in the life of The Gov."

The most amazing point of that trip is that I almost didn't go. It was very difficult to be away at that time because of several pressing circumstances. I went out of the sheer conviction that He had opened up this opportunity to me. I'm not called to "Lopland" but my friends are. Being there with their children provided them the opportunity to learn the language which is imperative for them to be effective. I knew I was to go and serve them in whatever capacity I could. I can truthfully say, I have never felt more fulfilled on any other trip abroad than this one. I spent a great deal of time in the kitchen cooking and with the boys, and an even greater amount of time being happy.

There was a struggle greater than words in saying "yes" to this trip. It wasn't the going that was hard but the leaving of Dad. My friend Stephanie spent an entire evening with me on my couch as I sobbed with the struggle to say "yes." In addition I had such an intense battle with fear. I have never been afraid of flying, but this time I strongly suspected I might die. I made sure my mother had my life insurance policy and knew where my will was. Again, I was sobbing and out of control when I told my family good-bye. Of course that really made them feel good about me going. The only reason I share the dramatics of my story is to reiterate that we can't always obey out of our feelings or convenience. Whether it is off to another country or down to the homeless shelter, it is the love of Christ that compels us to give and to daily die to self. In listening to an account of the life of St. Margeret, the beloved Queen of Scotland, I was so provoked by the life she lived, characterized by love. As their queen she washed the feet of the sick and destitute. She died in 1093, and it was said of her life that she "died daily" as she sacrificially served her people as their queen and as a servant.

Many years ago I wrote a prayer in my journal that I sometimes think I should cross-stitch so that I can see it daily. "Let the 'I' in my life look like 'i'. Sometimes I feel like I am 'i', but most of the time it is 'I' right out there front and center. "The Kingdom of Angela." May I encourage you to always remember that it is only through His amazing grace that He uses any of us. What a wonderful way to look at life.

For when we think we can do anything on our own, we easily lose sight of whom we are dependent upon. We pray our desire is to be: "Lord keep us ever mindful of our need of Thee."

May each of us come to that place, surrender, and see the world through His eyes. Sometimes the first step is "Lord, I am willing to be willing." He doesn't drag us around to do His will, but He walks along beside us and encourages us along the way. You are not alone on this journey. For the very One that desires that you live as an extension of Him is the One that has called you. "You shall go out with joy and be led forth with peace" (Isa. 55:12). I have a feeling you are going to enjoy the journey!

LIVING TO DIE
(Epilogue)

The morning summer sun was on our faces as my nieces and I walked outside. Both of their little hands were in mine and we strolled slowly so Lydia, the younger, could keep up with Caroline and me. In the middle of the field adjoining my parents' yard, we stopped and looked up into the sky. I knelt beside them and their eyes looked expectantly into mine. Then we watched quietly as the balloons we had brought with us slowly and gently lifted into the morning breeze. Tears streamed down my face. The gentle bouncing of heavenly colors of yellow, white, and blue were a lovely contrast in the cloudless sky. This was a day when colors would be meaningful to me.

Caroline and Lydia didn't quite understand where their "G-daddy" had gone. We had talked about heaven, but I wondered where heaven was in their young minds. In the final battle for my father's life only a few days before, I had felt the tangible coldness of death surrounding my family. Yet in the closing hours, we had known the sweetness of grieving with hope and not despair. The simple act of releasing the balloons to go to heaven with their grandfather brought a childlike understanding of heaven to these little girls, as well as to me. Kneeling with my arms around them, I felt the sacredness of the moment.

That day I so identified with the words of Ann Kiemel Anderson after her own father's death: "I am deeply changed and forever quieted and humbled by life, by its gifts and the quickness by which it can be snapped away." Like Ann, my experience with death on a personal level made me more convinced than ever that we should constantly strive to improve what is so casually referred to as our "quality of life."

We would be wise to realize that our years, our days, and our hours are a gift from God alone. Our times, our words, our conversations, our business activities, and all that we do are a gift from Him. With this truth engraved upon our hearts, we should cherish every breath and live each day with gratefulness. Each second of our lives is closer to that which is eternal. That is why we were given life in the first place. In essence, we are living to die.

As single women, this is a wonderful time to evaluate the activities of our fleeting lives. We can live life exhausted and self-centered, or we can continually refresh ourselves in His presence and seek to share His life with others. May our daily prayer be, "Teach us to number our days so that we might present to Thee a heart of wisdom, and that we might have wisdom in ordering the moments of our days." Then when we do make our final journey, we can say, "It is well with my soul," instead of, "Oh, I needed to pick up one more thing at the mall."

While Dietrich Bonhoeffer was being led away to his execution on the morning of April 9, 1945, his last reported words were, "This is the end—for me the beginning—of life." What a wonderful outlook when a noose is hanging around your neck! Please do not think that I want for you to be morbid; on the contrary, I want for you to stop postponing the joy of living! As Nicole Johnson says in *Fresh Brewed Life*, "A lot of us are not afraid of dying. We're afraid of living. We don't know what we are living for." Living a life with purpose doesn't just happen haphazardly. It takes the desire and commitment to evaluate what is really meaningful and worthy of your time and emotion. Take time to think about living so that you are not wasting the moments that are passing so quickly.

The very One who has given us life is the One to whom we can entrust it without hesitation or reservation. In the wake of young John F. Kennedy's fatal plane crash, much attention was given to the topic of flight disorientation, the probable cause of Kennedy's accident. This tragedy prompted some reflections I thought were worth my paying attention to. I sent an email to my good friend Dave Franz, a flight inspector of safety for the U.S. Air Force: "Dave, in laywoman's terminology, please describe what happens as a pilot gets in trouble—let's say bad weather conditions. From what I understand, in the event of disorientation or hazardous weather, it is in the pilot's best interest to look at the instrument panel and not outside the window. Please give me some insight. I have a feeling there is a lesson I can learn."

Major Franz did not comply with my request to keep it simple; his reply was in *Top Gun* lingo about somotogravic sensations and so forth. However, the bottom line answer was this: "Your sensory perceptions can get you into serious trouble in seconds if you pay more attention to them than to the instrument panel. Unfortunately, you could be upside down plunging toward *terra firma* or water and *feel* like you were sitting upright in your seat." I confirmed with him later that even in the most horrific flying conditions you might feel as if you need to pull your parachute chord when really everything is right on course. Now who in the world does that remind you of? It is indeed a parallel to our lives, as we come to that place of keeping our eyes on the control panel and not looking out the window.

How many times in assessing the weather conditions of my life have I panicked and fumbled for the eject button while clutching my parachute chord? And really my life was right on course, despite the turbulence. Perhaps you are in a storm and hear the alarms of panic screaming as you feel yourself plummeting to what feels like the center of the earth. Or perhaps you really are spiraling downward and are too busy enjoying the hazy clouds to notice.

Why do we delay our trust in God or question His wisdom? In our minds we know it is outrageous for us to think that our wisdom exceeds the Lord's. And yet, when we have the opportunity to trust, we waver and want to think about it for a while. How many times have you placed your life with confidence into the hands of someone you didn't know? Any means of public transportation requires the transference of trust into the hands of the operator. I have never personally known the pilot or conductor of a plane or train I was riding, and most likely you haven't either. Why in the world would we entrust our lives to someone we don't know, when even the slightest misjudgment on their parts could result in our death? And yet with our own Heavenly Father, we so often foolishly demand our own way, forgetting temporarily that there will be consequences.

One of my favorite old hymns identifies our whole Christian duty in a single imperative: "Trust and obey, for there's no other way to be happy in Jesus but to trust and obey." It is really a simple equation. It's when we throw in the other factors of procrastination, our time table, and the desire to understand that we crash. But my heart continues to trust God, for the very One to whom I have entrusted my life is the One who knows me better than I know myself. One of my life verses is from Psalm 31:5, "My times are in your hands," and I often find myself thinking of His hands. I see them as warm and embracing, very gentle, and certainly big enough to hold all of me in them. All of my inner longings, desires, and the brokenness as well.

In the moments of crushing or blinding disappointments, when I have responded with a heart that said "I choose to trust you," hope has been restored. I have often recalled the words of Betsie Ten Boom to her sister Corrie at the concentration camp of Ravensbruck: "There are no *ifs* in God's world and no places that are safer than other places. The center of His will is our hiding place." Helen Keller seemed to exhibit a similar attitude of trust and thankfulness. "So much has been given to me," she wrote" that I have no time to ponder over that which has been denied."

Only a few months before she died, Mother Teresa took the time to write to an aspiring songwriter. Her godly counsel to him voices the same desire for my life. "Whatever you do—whether to carve a door or to write a song that God inspires you to write—do it all for His glory and the good of His people. Always do small things with great love, and be ready to take whatever He gives and give whatever He takes with a big smile." Her words reaffirmed to me the truth from Proverbs 31: "She smiles at the future." Because of Him, our futures are secure and we can smile. Though we sometimes don't feel like beaming about our life circumstances, if our heart attitude is one of trust and gratefulness, we will see our surroundings with new eyes and a bigger heart.

When we stand before the Lord at the end of our lives, the question will not be, "Were you married?" But rather, "What have you done with God's gift of life to you?" Every moment that He gives to you as a single woman (and perhaps one day as a married one) is to be lived for a purpose beyond yourself. Trust Him. Keep Him foremost in your heart. God will take the moments that make up our minutes, days, and hours and fill them with the fullness of His life. Be assured that as you are about your Father's business, He will be busy about all the things that concern you. I pray that you will hear Him say to you, "Let there be life in every breath, and may you live it freely and confidently, every single moment."

Acknowledgements

I think my mother thought that when she gave birth to me her labor pains were over. Little did she know they were just beginning. I'm sorry that Dr. Dobson had not yet written *The Strong Willed Child* when I came along! It has been her prayers most of all, that have contributed to this venture. As found in Proverbs 31, this daughter rises up and calls you blessed. To my mother, Irene Grace, I love you dearly.

Many warm and loving thoughts to my sisters Sunnie and Shawn who are my friends as well as exemplary wives and mothers. I used to be so proud to have my little sisters visit me in grammar school, and now I look to you for advice and encouragement. You know me, and you love me. Amazing. Thanks for marrying two fabulous men, Shane Henry and Brian Cagle, who happen to be my favorite brothers-in-law.

To Caroline, Lydia, and all other future little ones, your Sissy is *crazy* about her favorite honey buns! How wonderful for God to choose *me* to be your auntie! You bring joy-filled delight, laughter, and wonder to my life. I am happy to announce that James Luke Cagle arrived just in time to get his name added. He is seven pounds and eleven ounces of sweetness, and I'm already in love with the little guy.

Granted this book that you are holding has my name on it, but many lives have been intricately involved in its composition, some in the actual writing process and all as a continuous source of encouragement and refreshment. The circle of people that have shaped my life encompasses me, and for each I am grateful. Unfortunately, it is not possible for me to acknowledge each for that list would be longer than the book itself.

Tara Springfield—Thank you for the phone call that started all of this. From that Passover night to a book...who would have imagined?! You are a faithful and cherished friend. You are integrally woven into this book because of your consistent encouragement, insightful perspective, and many prayers.

Delma Mitchell—You were the very first to read my thoughts there on your wonderful Mississippi farm. You were right. He did take care of all the little details! How grateful I am for Boatmanville and your special family.

Jack Cunningham—Surprise! I finally listened to you! Your notes of encouragement over the years remain in the archives of special treasures. Thank you, dear Jack.

Stephanie Grissom—You kept the flame to this vision kindled when I was ready to blow it out, long before there was ever a book contract. Those hours of prayer have had incredible dividends. I got a book, and you got a husband! And by the way, thanks for picking one that took me in as part of the package deal! My heart-felt gratitude and love to both you and Terry and for the investment of many hours of reading during rewrites. I appreciate your insight and prayerful suggestions during those final deadlines and for staying calm when I wasn't. No more of this silly little people talk! Chicago in the fall?!

When I cook I rarely follow a recipe. I open and pour and throw in and stir. It usually turns out great. That is how I went about writing this book, and it was disaster—a big mess. I had eighteen years of journals and lots of piles of papers. Fortunately for me, there are two people in this world who not only are gifted in writing as professors but are the types of friends spoken of in the book of John, the greatest love is shown when a person gives of themselves for their friends. Mary Virginia Sommer and Ruth Northcutt spent seven weeks poring through endless piles of my papers. Their husbands were extremely forbearing and benevolent as they shared their wives with me. I want to thank Ron Sommer and Scott Northcutt. Not only did the Sommers open their hearts to me but their home as well, daily exemplifying the characteristics of St. Paul as they endured my "lightning rod" experiences. Although Baby Paola cannot yet read (even though you are a Wonder) thanks for sharing your mother with me. Mary Virginia, my heart is filled with gratefulness as I remember you over the computer late at night and our endless cups of Italian cappuccino. I will always be grateful to God for bringing our lives together those many years ago, and I cherish our friendship. May He bless this child within you with grace and blessings. Again to Ruth, thank you my dear, for walking along this journey with me through emails and countless phone calls and your wise and gentle advice.

My thanks to John D. and Gemma Reese who encouraged and prayed for me during those weeks and spent many hours baby-sitting. Dr. Paola Reese graciously filled in as my interim physician and took care of my sprained ankle (the one that happened when I fell out of the door while writing about gracefulness) and my other assorted medical crises. My thanks to Linda Brown from whose door I fell as she opened up her little pink house to me with warm hospitality. Thank you all for your love, patience and prayers.

Dr. Maxx Abraham—How proud I am to call you The Prof! You are indeed the paradigm of the Maximized Man! I am still in awe that you missed the World Series to coach me through another computer crisis. I am grateful for the many times you convinced me that throwing my computer through the window would not solve anything, as well as continuously encouraging me in this project. My one comfort is that I have helped in grooming you in the fine art of dealing with female hysteria. This knowledge should be beneficial to you in the future. Get busy.

Dorothy Sewell—I think of you and I smile. I call you D&B friend. You will understand and you are, you know.

Dena Lowry—Your friendship is one of my favorite things that happened to me in Jerusalem. Your unconditional love is a delight to my heart.

Karen Berger—The God of Israel who never sleeps shall continue to keep you my precious friend, in His Beloved Land. Blessings on all your dreams.

Roger and Maureen Salter—How I have loved our fireside chats together and with God. I'm grateful that you and your children obediently crossed the Atlantic Ocean so that many would know that special love and warmth of His love that you share. Thank you for your heart and vision for my life.

Of the many threads of grace and love woven into my life I cannot fail to mention Joe and Wrae Fowler who were my first spiritual parents. They have walked faithfully beside me for many years always loving me unconditionally. Gladys and Jerry Funk and Victor and Dottie Marden are also part of my spiritual parentage as they have lovingly and faithfully guided me in so many stages of my life.

Miss Helen Wright—Happy Ninety Years of Life! You have truly lived every single moment and continue to with joy. I'm so grateful to be one of your many children.

There is a lovely-hearted student at Auburn University who has poured her young life into tender places of mine as I have watched her "grow up." Thank you dear Virginia Bradley, for coming and sleeping under the stars of CFO camp with me this past summer, as together we pondered heaven and life. May you always know His fullness of joy in all you do.

Helen Brock—Your perspective and heart for this book have been so invaluable to me. Thank you for your many hours of reading and your wise observations. You are a treasured blessing and I love praying with you and watching our prayers answered.

My Liberty Church family has been such an important part of my life. There are too many to name. My endearing thanks to my pastor Bruce Terry, Bob and Loretta Adams, Mark and Gemma Fowler, Jack Marshall, Roslyn Raley, Leslie Cope and Dee Dee Marler. Jim and Linda Ritchey and my wonderful home group have prayed so faithfully with such love and enthusiasm for this project. Thanks to Dr. Emmanuel Chekwa—a lousy painter but a most wonderful friend and counselor, for taking on the rather daunting task of helping me in time management. I wish you all the success!

Thanks to Shelley Kaylor—my friend who loved me enough to name her first daughter after me and has prayed for me so faithfully across the years and oceans that have separated us.

Ginger Ryan Combs—From that providential meeting in the bathroom at Briarwood Ballet through our many years and many seasons. How grateful I am for you. It's even okay that we never made it on stage! I'll dance with you anywhere my friend.

Mr. Harold Brown died in his eighty-seventh year of life while helping his neighbor: me. That was just like him…always helping. I feel sure he is in heaven playing his viola. Mrs. Mary Brown continues to make me smile as I enjoy the melody of her life from within and as she shares her love for classical music.

The following names are not just a list of people. They have each played a special part in my life in a significant way at various seasons of my life, and it's stressing me out not to write about each individually! Ann Dix, Lisa Horton, Tammy Fliesher, Cathy Carlson, Molly Bradley, Dave Franz, Melinda McGrath, Mensor Chadwick Sandra Bradley, Steve Skinner, Cindy Moseley, Dr. David and Lucy Wilson, Lanette Stone, Bill Barrett, Scott Austin, Dr. Victor Agbabor, Pamela Norton, Dr. Jim and Linda Boyce, Jeff Adams, Bonnie Smith, Dr. Jonathan (the blind date disaster!) and Christy Hood, Mark Shelton, Dee Dee Stephens, Amy Smith, Susannah Fowler, Candyce McGowan, Dave Roberts, Elizabeth and Thomas George, David Hambright, Earle and Judy Carpenter, Jim Harrison, Bella Imas, Vanessa Vienna, Jean Madden (my perennial friend) Daniel and Gwen Cason, and all of my many wonderful friends at Baptist Princeton Hospital.

This is my first experience with a publishing company and it has been most pleasant. To my new friends at New Hope Publishers, may I say how grateful I am to each of you. You have been encouraging, supportive, and oh so patient! My warm thanks to Coy Batson, Lynn Waldrep, Rachael Crutchfield, Amy Montgomery, and again Tara Springfield. My thanks to the nameless New Hope readers that critiqued my manuscript and the others involved whom I have not yet met. How grateful I am for the prayerful and wise guidance of my editor Leslie Caldwell. It has been such a pleasure working with you all.

And to you my reader, thank you for taking the time to read my thoughts. Please know that I am aware that many of them are simply my opinion. That's the nice thing about opinions, there are enough to go around and for everyone to have one. I would love to hear from you. You can contact me at: Angela Payne, P.O. Box 59881, Birmingham, AL 35259-9881.

To all the others that have prayed and encouraged me not only in relation to this writing project but along this journey called Life: You know who you are and you are in my heart. Always.

167

And most of all to my Lord Jesus Christ do I give thanks. He is the one I love and trust with all my heart...every single moment. I offer to Him my praise and thanksgiving for life that is not only present but forever and ever.